Letters on the Aesthetical Education of Man

by
Frederich Schiller

G P
GRINDL PRESS

This edition contains the complete and unabridged manuscript of *Letters on the Aesthetical Education of Man,* by Frederich Schiller. All content not in the public domain is original to this edition. Content in the public domain includes the manuscript and all images. Published in this translation in the Harvard Classics, edited by Charles W. Eliot, 1909.

ISBN: 978-1519782946

GP

GRINDL PRESS
grindlpress.com

from the
Classic Thought
Series
from Grindl Press

Titles of all series from Grindl Press
available for purchase at
www.grindlpress.com

Other Series

Contemporary Editions
Standard Classics
Drama Classics
Classic Short Story Collections
Classic Biography
Mystery Classics
Vocabulary From the Classics
Ethnic Studies
Regional Classics
Old West Classics
American Frontier Series
Classic History
Secondary Student Editions
College Editions
Classic Crafts
Classic Recipes
Classics for Young Adults
Classics for Children

CONTENTS

Letters on the
Aesthetical Education of Man

Letter I

By your permission I lay before you, in a series of letters, the results of my researches upon *beauty* and *art*. I am keenly sensible of the importance as well as of the charm and dignity of this undertaking. I shall treat a subject which is closely connected with the better portion of our happiness and not far removed from the moral nobility of human nature. I shall plead this cause of the beautiful before a heart by which her whole power is felt and exercised, and which will take upon itself the most difficult part of my task in an investigation where one is compelled to appeal as frequently to feelings as to principles.

That which I would beg of you as a favor, you generously impose upon me as a duty; and, when I solely consult my inclination, you impute to me a service. The liberty of action you prescribe is rather a necessity for me than a constraint. Little exercised in formal rules, I shall scarcely incur the risk of sinning against good taste by any undue use of them; my ideas, drawn rather from within than from reading or from an intimate experience with the world, will not disown their origin; they would rather incur any reproach than that of a sectarian bias, and would prefer to succumb by their innate feebleness than sustain themselves by borrowed authority and foreign support.

In truth, I will not keep back from you that the assertions which follow rest chiefly upon Kantian principles; but if in the course of these researches you should be reminded of any special school of philosophy, ascribe it to my incapacity, not to those principles. No; your liberty of mind shall be sacred to me; and the facts upon which I build will be furnished by your own sentiments; your own unfettered thought will dictate the laws according to which we have to proceed.

With regard to the ideas which predominate in the practical part of Kant's system, philosophers only disagree, whilst mankind, I am confident of proving, have never done so. If stripped of their technical shape, they will appear as the verdict of reason pronounced from time immemorial by common consent, and as facts of the moral instinct which nature, in her wisdom, has given to man in order to serve as guide and teacher until his enlightened intelligence gives him maturity. But this very technical shape which renders truth visible to the understanding conceals it from the feelings; for, unhappily, understanding begins by destroying the object of the inner sense before it can appropriate the object. Like the chemist, the philosopher finds synthesis only by analysis, or the spontaneous work of nature only through the torture of art. Thus, in order to detain the fleeting apparition, he must enchain it in the fetters of rule, dissect its fair proportions into abstract notions, and preserve its living spirit in a fleshless skeleton of words. Is it surprising that natural feeling should not recognize itself in such a copy, and if in the report of the analyst the truth appears as paradox?

Permit me therefore to crave your indulgence if the following researches should remove their object from the sphere of sense while endeavoring to draw it towards the

Letters on the Aesthetical Education of Man

understanding. That which I before said of moral experience can be applied with greater truth to the manifestation of "the beautiful." It is the mystery which enchants, and its being is extinguished with the extinction of the necessary combination of its elements.

Letter II

But I might perhaps make a better use of the opening you afford me if I were to direct your mind to a loftier theme than that of art. It would appear to be unseasonable to go in search of a code for the aesthetic world, when the moral world offers matter of so much higher interest, and when the spirit of philosophical inquiry is so stringently challenged by the circumstances of our times to occupy itself with the most perfect of all works of art — the establishment and structure of a true political freedom.

It is unsatisfactory to live out of your own age and to work for other times. It is equally incumbent on us to be good members of our own age as of our own state or country. If it is conceived to be unseemly and even unlawful for a man to segregate himself from the customs and manners of the circle in which he lives, it would be inconsistent not to see that it is equally his duty to grant a proper share of influence to the voice of his own epoch, to its taste and its requirements, in the operations in which he engages.

But the voice of our age seems by no means favorable to art, at all events to that kind of art to which my inquiry is directed. The course of events has given a direction to the genius of the time that threatens to remove it continually further from the ideal of art. For art has to leave reality, it has to raise itself boldly above necessity and neediness; for art is the daughter of freedom, and it requires its prescriptions and rules to be furnished by the necessity of spirits and not by that of matter. But in our day it is necessity, neediness, that prevails, and lends a degraded humanity under its iron yoke. *Utility* is the great idol of the time, to which all powers do homage and all subjects are subservient. In this great balance on utility, the spiritual service of art has no weight, and, deprived of all encouragement, it vanishes from the noisy Vanity Fair of our time. The very spirit of philosophical inquiry itself robs the imagination of one promise after another, and the frontiers of art are narrowed in proportion as the limits of science are enlarged.

The eyes of the philosopher as well as of the man of the world are anxiously turned to the theatre of political events, where it is presumed the great destiny of man is to be played out. It would almost seem to betray a culpable indifference to the welfare of society if we did not share this general interest. For this great commerce in social and moral principles is of necessity a matter of the greatest concern to every human being, on the ground both of its subject and of its results. It must accordingly be of deepest moment to every man to think for himself. It would seem that now at length a question that formerly was only settled by the law of the stronger is to be determined by the calm judgment of the reason, and every man who is capable of placing himself in a central position, and raising his individuality into that of his species, can look upon himself as in possession of this judicial faculty of reason; being moreover, as man and member of the human family, a party in the case under trial and involved more or less in its decisions. It would thus appear that this great political process is not only engaged with his individual case, it has also to pronounce enactments, which he as a rational spirit is capable of enunciating and entitled to pronounce.

It is evident that it would have been most attractive to me to inquire into an object such as this, to decide such a question in conjunction with a thinker of powerful mind, a man of liberal sympathies, and a heart imbued with a noble enthusiasm for the weal of humanity. Though so widely separated by worldly position, it would have been a delightful surprise to have found your unprejudiced mind arriving at the same result as my own in the field of ideas. Nevertheless, I think I can not only excuse, but even justify by solid grounds, my step in resisting this attractive purpose and in preferring beauty to freedom. I hope that I shall succeed in convincing you that this matter of art is less foreign to the needs than to the tastes of our age; nay, that, to arrive at a solution even in the political problem, the road of aesthetics must be pursued, because it is through beauty that we arrive at freedom. But I cannot carry out this proof without my bringing to your remembrance the principles by which the reason is guided in political legislation.

Letter III

Man is not better treated by nature in his first start than her other works are; so long as he is unable to act for himself as an independent intelligence she acts for him. But the very fact that constitutes him a man is that he does not remain stationary, where nature has placed him, that he can pass with his reason, retracing the steps nature had made him anticipate, that he can convert the work of necessity into one of free solution, and elevate physical necessity into a moral law.

When man is raised from his slumber in the senses he feels that he is a man; he surveys his surroundings and finds that he is in a state. He was introduced into this state by the power of circumstances, before he could freely select his own position. But as a moral being he cannot possibly rest satisfied with a political condition forced upon him by necessity, and only calculated for that condition; and it would be unfortunate if this did satisfy him. In many cases man shakes off this blind law of necessity, by his free spontaneous action, of which among many others we have an instance, in his ennobling by beauty and suppressing by moral influence the powerful impulse implanted in him by nature in the passion of love. Thus, when arrived at maturity, he recovers his childhood by an artificial process, he founds a state of nature in his ideas, not given him by any experience, but established by the necessary laws and conditions of his reason, and he attributes to this ideal condition an object, an aim, of which he was not cognizant in the actual reality of nature. He gives himself a choice of which he was not capable before, and sets to work just as if he were beginning anew, and were exchanging his original state of bondage for one of complete independence, doing this with complete insight and of his free decision. He is justified in regarding this work of political thraldom as non-existing, though a wild and arbitrary caprice may have founded its work very artfully; though it may strive to maintain it with great arrogance and encompass it with a halo of veneration. For the work of blind powers possesses no authority before which freedom need bow, and all must be made to adapt itself to the highest end which reason has set up in his personality. It is in this wise that a people in a state of manhood is justified in exchanging a condition of thraldom for one of moral freedom.

Now the term natural condition can be applied to every political body which owes its establishment originally to forces and not to laws, and such a state contradicts the moral nature of man, because lawfulness can alone have authority over this. At the same time this natural condition is quite sufficient for the physical man, who only gives himself laws in order to get rid of brute force. Moreover, the physical man is a *reality*, and the moral man *problematical*. Therefore when the reason suppresses the natural condition, as she must if she wishes to substitute her own, she weighs the real physical man against the problematical moral man, she weighs the existence of society against a possible, though morally necessary, ideal of society. She takes from man something which he really possesses, and without which he possesses nothing, and refers him as a substitute to something that he ought to possess and might possess; and if reason had relied too exclusively on him she might, in order to secure him a state of humanity in which he is wanting and can want without injury to his life, have robbed him even of the means of animal existence, which is the first necessary *condition* of his being a man. Before he had opportunity to hold firm to the law with his will, reason would have withdrawn from his feet the ladder of nature.

The great point is, therefore, to reconcile these two considerations, to prevent physical society from ceasing for a moment *in time*, while the moral society is being formed in the *idea*; in other words, to prevent its existence from being placed in jeopardy for the sake of the moral dignity of man. When the mechanic has to mend a watch he lets the wheels run out; but the living watchworks of the state have to be repaired while they act, and a wheel has to be exchanged for another during its revolutions. Accordingly props must be sought for to support society and keep it going while it is made independent of the natural condition from which it is sought to emancipate it.

This prop is not found in the natural character of man, who, being selfish and violent, directs his energies rather to the destruction than to the preservation of society. Nor is it found in his moral character, which has to be formed, which can never be worked upon or calculated on by the lawgiver, because it is free and *never appears*. It would seem, therefore, that another measure must be adopted. It would seem that the physical character of the arbitrary must be separated from moral freedom; that it is incumbent to make the former harmonize with the laws and the latter dependent on impressions; it would be expedient to remove the former still farther from matter and to bring the latter somewhat more near to it; in short, to produce a third character related to both the others—the physical and the moral—paving the way to a transition from the sway of mere force to that of law, without preventing the proper development of the moral character, but serving rather as a pledge in the sensuous sphere of a morality in the unseen.

Letter IV

Thus much is certain. It is only when a third character, as previously suggested, has preponderance that a revolution in a state according to moral principles can be free from injurious consequences; nor can anything else secure its endurance. In proposing or setting up a moral state, the moral law is relied upon as a real power, and free-will is drawn into the realm of causes, where all hangs together mutually with stringent necessity and rigidity. But we know that the condition of the human will always remains contingent, and that only in the Absolute Being physical coexists with moral necessity. Accordingly, if it is wished to depend on the moral conduct of man as on natural results, this conduct must become nature, and he must be led by natural impulse to such a course of action as can only and invariably have moral results. But the will of man is perfectly free between inclination and duty, and no physical necessity ought to enter as a sharer in this magisterial personality. If, therefore, he is to retain this power of solution, and yet become a reliable link in the causal concatenation of forces, this can only be effected when the operations of both these impulses are presented quite equally in the world of appearances. It is only possible when, with every difference of form, the matter of man's volition remains the same, when all his impulses agreeing with his reason are sufficient to have the value of a universal legislation.

It may be urged that every individual man carries within himself, at least in his adaptation and destination, a purely ideal man. The great problem of his existence is to bring all the incessant changes of his outer life into conformity with the unchanging unity of this ideal. This pure ideal man, which makes itself known more or less clearly in every subject, is represented by the state, which is the objective, and, so to speak, canonical form in which the manifold differences of the subjects strive to unite. Now two ways present themselves to the thought in which the man of time can agree with the man of idea, and there are also two ways in which the state can maintain itself in individuals. One of these ways is when the pure ideal man subdues the empirical man, and the state suppresses the individual, or again when the individual *becomes the state*, and the man of time is *ennobled* to the man of *idea*.

I admit that in a one-sided estimate from the point of view of morality this difference vanishes, for the reason is satisfied if her law prevails unconditionally. But when the survey taken is complete and embraces the whole man (anthropology), where the form is considered together with the substance, and a living feeling has a voice, the difference will become far more evident. No doubt the reason demands unity, and nature variety, and both legislations take man in hand. The law of the former is stamped upon him by an incorruptible consciousness, that of the latter by an ineradicable feeling. Consequently education will always appear deficient when the moral feeling can only be maintained with the sacrifice of what is natural; and a political administration will always be very imperfect when it is only able to bring about unity by suppressing variety. The state ought not only to respect the objective and generic, but also the subjective and specific in individuals; and while diffusing the unseen world of morals, it must not depopulate the kingdom of appearance, the external world of matter.

When the mechanical artist places his hand on the formless block, to give it a form according to his intention, he has not any scruples in doing violence to it. For the nature on which he works does not deserve any respect in itself, and he does not value the whole for its parts, but the parts on account of the whole. When the child of the fine arts sets his hand to the same block, he has no scruples either in doing violence to it, he only avoids showing this violence. He does not respect the matter in which he works any more than the mechanical artist; but he seeks by an apparent consideration for it to deceive the eye which takes this matter under its protection. The political and educating artist follows a very different course, while making man at once his material and his end. In this case the aim or end meets in the material, and it is only because the whole serves the parts that the parts adapt themselves to the end. The political artist has to treat his material—man—with a very different kind of respect than that shown by the artist of fine art to his work. He must spare man's peculiarity and personality, not to produce a defective effect on the senses, but objectively and out of consideration for his inner being.

But the state is an organization which fashions itself through itself and for itself, and for this reason it can only be realized when the parts have been accorded to the idea of the whole. The state serves the purpose of a representative, both to pure ideal and to objective humanity, in the breast of its citizens, accordingly it will have to observe the same relation to its citizens in which they are placed to it; and it will only respect their subjective humanity in the same degree that it is ennobled to an objective existence. If the internal man is one with himself he will be able to rescue his peculiarity, even in the greatest generalization of his conduct, and the state will only become the exponent of his fine instinct, the clearer formula of his internal legislation. But if the subjective man is in conflict with the objective, and contradicts him in the character of a people, so that only the oppression of the former can give victory to the latter, then the state will take up the severe aspect of the law against the citizen, and in order not to fall a sacrifice, it will have to crush under foot such a hostile individuality without any compromise.

Now man can be opposed to himself in a twofold manner; either as a savage, when his feelings rule over his principles; or as a barbarian, when his principles destroy his feelings. The savage despises art, and acknowledges nature as his despotic ruler; the barbarian laughs at nature, and dishonors it, but he often proceeds in a more contemptible way than the savage to be the slave of his senses. The cultivated man makes of nature his friend, and honors its friendship, while only bridling its caprice.

Consequently, when reason brings her moral unity into physical society, she must not injure the manifold in nature. When nature strives to maintain her manifold character in the moral structure of society, this must not create any breach in moral unity; the victorious form is equally remote from uniformity and confusion. Therefore, *totality* of character must be found in the people which is capable and worthy to exchange the state of necessity for that of freedom.

Letter V

Does the present age, do passing events, present this character? I direct my attention at once to the most prominent object in this vast structure.

It is true that the consideration of opinion is fallen; caprice is unnerved, and, although still armed with power, receives no longer any respect. Man has awakened from his long lethargy and self-deception, and he demands with impressive unanimity to be restored to his imperishable rights. But he does not only demand them; he rises on all sides to seize by force what, in his opinion, has been unjustly wrested from him. The edifice of the natural state is tottering, its foundations shake, and a physical possibility seems at length granted to place law on the throne, to honor man at length as an end, and to make true freedom the basis of political union. Vain hope! The moral possibility is wanting, and the generous occasion finds an unsusceptible rule.

Man paints himself in his actions, and what is the form depicted in the drama of the present time? On the one hand, he is seen running wild, on the other, in a state of lethargy; the two extremest stages of human degeneracy, and both seen in one and the same period.

In the lower larger masses, coarse, lawless impulses come to view, breaking loose when the bonds of civil order are burst asunder, and hastening with unbridled fury to satisfy their savage instinct. Objective humanity may have had cause to complain of the state; yet subjective man must honor its institutions. Ought he to be blamed because he lost sight of the dignity of human nature, so long as he was concerned in preserving his existence? Can we blame him that he proceeded to separate by the force of gravity, to fasten by the force of cohesion, at a time when there could be no thought of building or raising up? The extinction of the state contains its justification. Society set free, instead of hastening upward into organic life, collapses into its elements.

On the other hand, the civilized classes give us the still more repulsive sight of lethargy, and of a depravity of character which is the more revolting because it roots in culture. I forget who of the older or more recent philosophers makes the remark, that what is more noble is the more revolting in its destruction. The remark applies with truth to the world of morals. The child of nature, when he breaks loose, becomes a madman; but the art scholar, when he breaks loose, becomes a debased character. The enlightenment of the understanding, on which the more refined classes pride themselves with some ground, shows on the whole so little of an ennobling influence on the mind that it seems rather to confirm corruption by its maxims. We deny nature on her legitimate field and feel her tyranny in the moral sphere, and while resisting her impressions, we receive our principles from her. While the affected decency of our manners does not even grant to nature a pardonable influence in the initial stage, our materialistic system of morals allows her the casting vote in the last and essential stage. Egotism has founded its system in the very bosom of a refined society, and without developing even a sociable character, we feel all the contagions and miseries of society. We subject our free judgment to its despotic opinions, our feelings to its bizarre customs, and our will to its seductions. We only maintain our caprice against her holy rights. The man of the world has his heart contracted by a proud self-complacency, while that of the man of nature often beats in sympathy; and every man seeks for nothing more than to save his wretched property from the general destruction, as it were from some great conflagration. It is conceived that the only way to find a shelter against the aberrations of sentiment is by completely foregoing its indulgence, and mockery, which is often a useful chastener of mysticism, slanders in the same breath the noblest aspirations. Culture, far from giving us freedom, only develops, as it advances, new necessities; the fetters of the physical close more tightly around us, so that the fear of loss quenches even the ardent impulse toward improvement, and the maxims of passive obedience are held to be the highest wisdom of life. Thus the spirit of the time is seen to waver between perversion and savagism, between what is unnatural and mere nature, between superstition and moral unbelief, and it is often nothing but the equilibrium of evils that sets bounds to it.

Letter VI

Have I gone too far in this portraiture of our times? I do not anticipate this stricture, but rather another—that I have proved too much by it. You will tell me that the picture I have presented resembles the humanity of our day, but it also bodies forth all nations engaged in the same degree of culture, because all, without exception, have fallen off from nature by the abuse of reason, before they can return to it through reason.

But if we bestow some serious attention to the character of our times, we shall be astonished at the contrast between the present and the previous form of humanity, especially that of Greece. We are justified in claiming the reputation of culture and refinement, when contrasted with a purely natural state of society, but not so comparing ourselves with the Grecian nature. For the latter was combined with all the charms of art and with all the dignity of wisdom, without, however, as with us, becoming a victim to these influences. The Greeks have put us to shame not only by their simplicity, which is foreign to our age; they are at the same time our rivals, nay, frequently our models, in those very points of superiority from which we seek comfort when regretting the unnatural character of our manners. We see that remarkable people uniting at once fulness of form and fulness of substance, both philosophizing and creating, both tender and energetic, uniting a youthful fancy to the virility of reason in a glorious humanity.

At the period of Greek culture, which was an awakening of the powers of the mind, the senses and the spirit had no distinctly separated property; no division had yet torn them asunder, leading them to partition in a hostile attitude, and to mark off their limits with precision. Poetry had not as yet become the adversary of wit, nor had speculation abused itself by passing into quibbling. In cases of necessity both poetry and wit could exchange parts, because they both honored truth only in their special way. However high might be the flight of reason, it drew matter in a loving spirit after it, and while sharply and stiffly defining it, never mutilated what it touched. It is true the Greek mind displaced humanity, and recast it on a magnified scale in the glorious circle of its gods; but it did this not by dissecting human nature, but by giving it fresh combinations, for the whole of human nature was represented in each of the gods. How different is the course followed by us moderns! We also displace and magnify individuals to form the image of the species, but we do this in a fragmentary way, not by altered combinations, so that it is necessary to gather up from different individuals the elements that form the species in its totality. It would almost appear as if the powers of mind express themselves with us in real life or empirically as separately as the psychologist distinguishes them in the representation. For we see not only individual subjects, but whole classes of men, uphold their capacities only in part, while the rest of their faculties scarcely show a germ of activity, as in the case of the stunted growth of plants.

I do not overlook the advantages to which the present race, regarded as a unity and in the balance of the understanding, may lay claim over what is best in the ancient world; but it is obliged to engage in the contest as a compact mass, and measure itself as a whole against a whole. Who among the moderns could step forth, man against man, and strive with an Athenian for the prize of higher humanity.

Whence comes this disadvantageous relation of individuals coupled with great advantages of the race? Why could the individual Greek be qualified as the type of his time; and why can no modern dare to offer himself as such? Because all-uniting nature imparted its forms to the Greek, and an all-dividing understanding gives our forms to us.

It was culture itself that gave these wounds to modern humanity. The inner union of human nature was broken, and a destructive contest divided its harmonious forces directly; on the one hand, an enlarged experience and a more distinct thinking necessitated a sharper separation of the sciences, while, on the other hand, the more complicated machinery of states necessitated a stricter sundering of ranks and occupations. Intuitive and speculative understanding took up a hostile attitude in opposite fields, whose borders were guarded with jealousy and distrust; and by limiting its operation to a narrow sphere, men have made unto themselves a master who is wont not unfrequently to end by subduing and oppressing all the other faculties. Whilst on the one hand a luxuriant imagination creates ravages in the plantations that have cost the intelligence so much labor; on the other hand, a spirit of abstraction suffocates the fire that might have warmed the heart and inflamed the imagination.

This subversion, commenced by art and learning in the inner man, was carried out to fulness and finished by the spirit of innovation in government. It was, no doubt, reasonable to expect that the simple organization of the primitive republics should survive the quaintness of primitive manners and of the relations of antiquity. But, instead of rising to a higher and nobler degree of animal life, this organization degenerated into a common and coarse mechanism. The zoophyte condition of the Grecian states, where each individual enjoyed an independent life, and could, in cases of necessity, become a separate whole and unit in himself, gave way to an ingenious mechanism, when, from the splitting up into numberless parts, there results a mechanical life in the combination. Then there was a rupture between the state and the church, between laws and customs; enjoyment was separated from labor, the means from the end, the effort from the reward. Man himself, eternally chained down to a little fragment of the whole, only forms a kind of fragment; having nothing in his ears but the monotonous sound of the perpetually revolving wheel, he never develops the harmony of his being, and instead of imprinting the seal of humanity on his being, he ends by being nothing more than the living impress of the craft to which he devotes himself, of the science that he cultivates. This very partial and paltry relation, linking the isolated members to the whole, does not depend on forms that are given spontaneously; for how could a complicated machine, which shuns the light, confide itself to the free will of man? This relation is rather dictated, with a rigorous strictness, by a formulary in which the free intelligence of man is chained down. The dead letter takes the place of a living meaning, and a practised memory becomes a safer guide than genius and feeling.

If the community or state measures man by his function, only asking of its citizens memory, or the intelligence of a craftsman, or mechanical skill, we cannot be surprised that the other faculties of the mind are neglected for the exclusive culture of the one that brings in honor and profit. Such is the necessary result of an organization that is indifferent about character, only looking to acquirements, whilst in other cases it tolerates the thickest darkness, to favor a spirit of law and order; it must result if it wishes that individuals in the exercise of special aptitudes should gain in depth what they are permitted to lose in extension. We are aware, no doubt, that a powerful genius does not shut up its activity within the limits of its functions; but mediocre talents consume in the craft fallen to their lot the whole of their feeble energy; and if some of their energy is reserved for matters of preference, without prejudice to its functions, such a state of things at once bespeaks a spirit soaring above the vulgar. Moreover, it is rarely a recommendation in the eye of a state to have a capacity superior to your employment, or one of those noble intellectual cravings of a man of talent which contend in rivalry with the duties of office. The state is so jealous of the exclusive possession of its servants that it would prefer—nor can it be blamed in this—for functionaries to show their powers with the Venus of Cytherea rather than the Uranian Venus.

It is thus that concrete individual life is extinguished, in order that the abstract whole may continue its miserable life, and the state remains forever a stranger to its citizens, because feeling does not discover it anywhere. The governing authorities find themselves compelled to classify, and thereby simplify the multiplicity of citizens, and only to know humanity in a representative form and at second-hand. Accordingly they end by entirely losing sight of humanity, and by confounding it with a simple artificial creation of the understanding, whilst on their part the subject-classes cannot help receiving coldly laws that address themselves so little to their personality. At length, society, weary of having a burden that the state takes so little trouble to lighten, falls to pieces and is broken up — a destiny that has long since attended most European states. They are dissolved in what may be called a state of moral nature, in which public authority is only one function more, hated and deceived by those who think it necessary, respected only by those who can do without it.

Thus compressed between two forces, within and without, could humanity follow any other course than that which it has taken? The speculative mind, pursuing imprescriptible goods and rights in the sphere of ideas, must needs have become a stranger to the world of sense, and lose sight of matter for the sake of form. On its part, the world of public affairs, shut up in a monotonous circle of objects, and even there restricted by formulas, was led to lose sight of the life and liberty of the whole, while becoming impoverished at the same time in its own sphere. Just as the speculative mind was tempted to model the real after the intelligible, and to raise the subjective laws of its imagination into laws constituting the existence of things, so the state spirit rushed into the opposite extreme, wished to make a particular and fragmentary experience the measure of all observation, and to apply without exception to all affairs the rules of its own particular craft. The speculative mind had necessarily to become the prey of a vain subtlety, the state spirit of a narrow pedantry; for the former was placed too high to see the individual, and the latter too low to survey the whole. But the disadvantage of this direction of mind was not confined to knowledge and mental production; it extended to action and feeling. We know that the sensibility of the mind depends, as to degree, on the liveliness, and for extent on the richness of the imagination. Now the predominance of the faculty of analysis must necessarily deprive the imagination of its warmth and energy, and a restricted sphere of objects must diminish its wealth. It is for this reason that the abstract thinker has very often a *cold* heart, because he analyzes impressions, which only move the mind by their combination or totality; on the other hand, the man of business, the statesman, has very often a narrow heart, because, shut up in the narrow circle of his employment, his imagination can neither expand nor adapt itself to another manner of viewing things.

My subject has led me naturally to place in relief the distressing tendency of the character of our own times and to show the sources of the evil, without its being my province to point out the compensations offered by nature. I will readily admit to you that, although this splitting up of their being was unfavorable for individuals, it was the only open road for the progress of the race. The point at which we see humanity arrived among the Greeks was undoubtedly a *maximum*; it could neither stop there nor rise higher. It could not stop there, for the sum of notions acquired forced infallibly the intelligence to break with feeling and intuition, and to lead to clearness of knowledge. Nor could it rise any higher; for it is only in a determinate measure that clearness can be reconciled with a certain degree of abundance and of warmth. The Greeks had attained this measure, and to continue their progress in culture, they, as we, were obliged to renounce the totality of their being, and to follow different and separate roads in order to seek after truth.

There was no other way to develop the manifold aptitudes of man than to bring them in opposition with one another. This antagonism of forces is the great instrument of culture, but it is only an instrument: for as long as this antagonism lasts man is only on the road to culture. It is only because these special forces are isolated in man, and because they take on themselves to impose all exclusive legislation, that they enter into strife with the truth of things, and oblige common sense, which generally adheres imperturbably to external phenomena, to dive into the essence of things. While pure understanding usurps authority in the world of sense, and empiricism attempts to subject this intellect to the conditions of experience, these two rival directions arrive at the highest possible development, and exhaust the whole extent of their sphere. While, on the one hand, imagination, by its tyranny, ventures to destroy the order of the world, it forces reason, on the other side, to rise up to the supreme sources of knowledge, and to invoke against this predominance of fancy the help of the law of necessity.

By an exclusive spirit in the case of his faculties, the individual is fatally led to error; but the species is led to truth. It is only by gathering up all the energy of our mind in a single focus, and concentrating a single force in our being, that we give in some sort wings to this isolated force, and that we draw it on artificially far beyond the limits that nature seems to have imposed upon it. If it be certain that all human individuals taken together would never have arrived, with the visual power given them by nature, to see a satellite of Jupiter, discovered by the telescope of the astronomer, it is just as well established that never would the human understanding have produced the analysis of the infinite, or the critique of pure reason, if in particular branches, destined for this mission, reason had not applied itself to special researches, and it, after having, as it were, freed itself from all matter, it had not, by the most powerful abstraction given to the spiritual eye of man the force necessary, in order to look into the absolute. But the question is, if a spirit thus absorbed in pure reason and intuition will be able to emancipate itself from the rigorous fetters of logic, to take the free action of poetry, and seize the individuality of things with a faithful and chaste sense? Here nature imposes even on the most universal genius a limit it cannot pass, and truth will make martyrs as long as philosophy will be reduced to make its principal occupation the search for arms against errors.

But whatever may be the final profit for the totality of the world, of this distinct and special perfecting of the human faculties, it cannot be denied that this final aim of the universe, which devotes them to this kind of culture, is a cause of suffering, and a kind of malediction for individuals. I admit that the exercises of the gymnasium form athletic bodies; but beauty is only developed by the free and equal play of the limbs. In the same way the tension of the isolated spiritual forces may make extraordinary men; but it is only the well-tempered equilibrium of these forces that can produce happy and accomplished men. And in what relation should we be placed with past and future ages if the perfecting of human nature made such a sacrifice indispensable? In that case we should have been the slaves of humanity, we should have consumed our forces in servile work for it during some thousands of years, and we should have stamped on our humiliated, mutilated nature the shameful brand of this slavery—all this in order that future generations, in a happy leisure, might consecrate themselves to the cure of their moral health, and develop the whole of human nature by their free culture.

But can it be true that man has to neglect himself for any end whatever? Can nature snatch from us, for any end whatever, the perfection which is prescribed to us by the aim of reason? It must be false that the perfecting of particular faculties renders the sacrifice of their totality necessary; and even if the law of nature had imperiously this tendency, we must have the power to reform by a superior art this totality of our being, which art has destroyed.

Letter VII

Can this effect of harmony be attained by the state? That is not possible, for the state, as at present constituted, has given occasion to evil, and the state as conceived in the idea, instead of being able to establish this more perfect humanity, ought to be based upon it. Thus the researches in which I have indulged would have brought me back to the same point from which they had called me off for a time. The present age, far from offering us this form of humanity, which we have acknowledged as a necessary condition of an improvement of the state, shows us rather the diametrically opposite form. If, therefore, the principles I have laid down are correct, and if experience confirms the picture I have traced of the present time, it would be necessary to qualify as unseasonable every attempt to effect a similar change in the state, and all hope as chimerical that would be based on such an attempt, until the division of the inner man ceases, and nature has been sufficiently developed to become herself the instrument of this great change and secure the reality of the political creation of reason.

In the physical creation, nature shows us the road that we have to follow in the moral creation. Only when the struggle of elementary forces has ceased in inferior organizations, nature rises to the noble form of the physical man. In like manner, the conflict of the elements of the moral man and that of blind instincts must have ceased, and a coarse antagonism in himself, before the attempt can be hazarded. On the other hand, the independence of man's character must be secured, and his submission to despotic forms must have given place to a suitable liberty, before the variety in his constitution can be made subordinate to the unity of the ideal. When the man of nature still makes such an anarchial abuse of his will, his liberty ought hardly to be disclosed to him. And when the man fashioned by culture makes so little use of his freedom, his free will ought not to be taken from him. The concession of liberal principles becomes a treason to social order when it is associated with a force still in fermentation, and increases the already exuberant energy of its nature. Again, the law of conformity under one level becomes tyranny to the individual when it is allied to a weakness already holding sway and to natural obstacles, and when it comes to extinguish the last spark of spontaneity and of originality.

The tone of the age must therefore rise from its profound moral degradation; on the one hand it must emancipate itself from the blind service of nature, and on the other it must revert to its simplicity, its truth, and its fruitful sap; a sufficient task for more than a century. However, I admit readily, more than one special effort may meet with success, but no improvement of the whole will result from it, and contradictions in action will be a continual protest against the unity of maxims. It will be quite possible, then, that in remote corners of the world humanity may be honored in the person of the negro, while in Europe it may be degraded in the person of the thinker. The old principles will remain, but they will adopt the dress of the age, and philosophy will lend its name to an oppression that was formerly authorized by the church. In one place, alarmed at the liberty which in its opening efforts always shows itself an enemy, it will cast itself into the arms of a convenient servitude. In another place, reduced to despair by a pedantic tutelage, it will be driven into the savage license of the state of nature. Usurpation will invoke the weakness of human nature, and insurrection will invoke its dignity, till at length the great sovereign of all human things, blind force, shall come in and decide, like a vulgar pugilist, this pretended contest of principles.

Letter VIII

Must philosophy therefore retire from this field, disappointed in its hopes? Whilst in all other directions the dominion of forms is extended, must this the most precious of all gifts be abandoned to a formless chance? Must the contest of blind forces last eternally in the political world, and is social law never to triumph over a hating egotism?

Not in the least. It is true that reason herself will never attempt directly a struggle with this brutal force which resists her arms, and she will be as far as the son of Saturn in the "Iliad" from descending into the dismal field of battle, to fight them in person. But she chooses the most deserving among the combatants, clothes him with divine arms as Jupiter gave them to his son-in-law, and by her triumphing force she finally decides the victory.

Reason has done all that she could in finding the law and promulgating it; it is for the energy of the will and the ardor of feeling to carry it out. To issue victoriously from her contest with force, truth herself must first become a force, and turn one of the instincts of man into her champion in the empire of phenomena. For instincts are the only motive forces in the material world. If hitherto truth has so little manifested her victorious power, this has not depended on the understanding, which could not have unveiled it, but on the heart which remained closed to it and on instinct which did not act with it.

Whence, in fact, proceeds this general sway of prejudices, this might of the understanding in the midst of the light disseminated by philosophy and experience? The age is enlightened, that is to say, that knowledge, obtained and vulgarized, suffices to set right at least on practical principles. The spirit of free inquiry has dissipated the erroneous opinions which long barred the access to truth, and has undermined the ground on which fanaticism and deception had erected their throne. Reason has purified itself from the illusions of the senses and from a mendacious sophistry, and philosophy herself raises her voice and exhorts us to return to the bosom of nature, to which she had first made us unfaithful. Whence then is it that we remain still barbarians?

There must be something in the spirit of man—as it is not in the objects themselves—which prevents us from receiving the truth, notwithstanding the brilliant light she diffuses, and from accepting her, whatever may be her strength for producing conviction. This something was perceived and expressed by an ancient sage in this very significant maxim: sapere aude [dare to be wise.]

Dare to be wise! A spirited courage is required to triumph over the impediments that the indolence of nature as well as the cowardice of the heart oppose to our instruction. It was not without reason that the ancient Mythos made Minerva issue fully armed from the head of Jupiter, for it is with warfare that this instruction commences. From its very outset it has to sustain a hard fight against the senses, which do not like to be roused from their easy slumber. The greater part of men are much too exhausted and enervated by their struggle with want to be able to engage in a new and severe contest with error. Satisfied if they themselves can escape from the hard labor of thought, they willingly abandon to others the guardianship of their thoughts. And if it happens that nobler necessities agitate their soul, they cling with a greedy faith to the formula that the state and the church hold in reserve for such cases. If these unhappy men deserve our compassion, those others deserve our just contempt, who, though set free from those necessities by more fortunate circumstances, yet willingly bend to their yoke. These latter persons prefer this twilight of obscure ideas, where the feelings have more intensity, and the imagination can at will create convenient chimeras, to the rays of truth which put to flight the pleasant illusions of their dreams. They have founded the whole structure of their happiness on these very illusions, which ought to be combated and dissipated by the light of knowledge, and they would think they were paying too dearly for a truth which begins by robbing them of all that has value in their sight. It would be necessary that they should be already sages to love wisdom: a truth that was felt at once by him to whom philosophy owes its name. [The Greek word means, as is known, love of wisdom.]

It is therefore not going far enough to say that the light of the understanding only deserves respect when it reacts on the character; to a certain extent it is from the character that this light proceeds; for the road that terminates in the head must pass through the heart. Accordingly, the most pressing need of the present time is to educate the sensibility, because it is the means, not only to render efficacious in practice the improvement of ideas, but to call this improvement into existence.

Letter IX

But perhaps there is a vicious circle in our previous reasoning! Theoretical culture must it seems bring along with it practical culture, and yet the latter must be the condition of the former. All improvement in the political sphere must proceed from the ennobling of the character. But, subject to the influence of a social constitution still barbarous, how can character become ennobled? It would then be necessary to seek for this end an instrument that the state does not furnish, and to open sources that would have preserved themselves pure in the midst of political corruption.

I have now reached the point to which all the considerations tended that have engaged me up to the present time. This instrument is the art of the beautiful; these sources are open to us in its immortal models.

Art, like science, is emancipated from all that is positive, and all that is humanly conventional; both are completely independent of the arbitrary will of man. The political legislator may place their empire under an interdict, but he cannot reign there. He can proscribe the friend of truth, but truth subsists; he can degrade the artist, but he cannot change art. No doubt, nothing is more common than to see science and art bend before the spirit of the age, and creative taste receive its law from critical taste. When the character becomes stiff and hardens itself, we see science severely keeping her limits, and art subject to the harsh restraint of rules; when the character is relaxed and softened, science endeavors to please and art to rejoice. For whole ages philosophers as well as artists show themselves occupied in letting down truth and beauty to the depths of vulgar humanity. They themselves are swallowed up in it; but, thanks to their essential vigor and indestructible life, the true and the beautiful make a victorious fight, and issue triumphant from the abyss.

No doubt the artist is the child of his time, but unhappy for him if he is its disciple or even its favorite! Let a beneficent deity carry off in good time the suckling from the breast of its mother, let it nourish him on the milk of a better age, and suffer him to grow up and arrive at virility under the distant sky of Greece. When he has attained manhood, let him come back, presenting a face strange to his own age; let him come, not to delight it with his apparition, but rather to purify it, terrible as the son of Agamemnon. He will, indeed, receive his matter from the present time, but he will borrow the form from a nobler time and even beyond all time, from the essential, absolute, immutable unity. There, issuing from the pure ether of its heavenly nature, flows the source of all beauty, which was never tainted by the corruptions of generations or of ages, which roll along far beneath it in dark eddies. Its matter may be dishonored as well as ennobled by fancy, but the ever-chaste form escapes from the caprices of imagination. The Roman had already bent his knee for long years to the divinity of the emperors, and yet the statues of the gods stood erect; the temples retained their sanctity for the eye long after the gods had become a theme for mockery, and the noble architecture of the palaces that shielded the infamies of Nero and of Commodus were a protest against them. Humanity has lost its dignity, but art has saved it, and preserves it in marbles full of meaning; truth continues to live in illusion, and the copy will serve to re-establish the model. If the nobility of art has *survived* the nobility of nature, it also goes before it like an inspiring genius, forming and awakening minds. Before truth causes her triumphant light to penetrate into the depths of the heart, poetry intercepts her rays, and the summits of humanity shine in a bright light, while a dark and humid night still hangs over the valleys.

But how will the artist avoid the corruption of his time which encloses him on all hands? Let him raise his eyes to his own dignity, and to law; let him not lower them to necessity and fortune. Equally exempt from a vain activity which would imprint its trace on the fugitive moment, and from the dreams of an impatient enthusiasm which applies the measure of the absolute to the paltry productions of time, let the artist abandon the real to the understanding, for that is its proper field. But let the artist endeavor to give birth to the ideal by the union of the possible and of the necessary. Let him stamp illusion and truth with the effigy of this ideal; let him apply it to the play of his imagination and his most serious actions, in short, to all sensuous and spiritual forms; then let him quietly launch his work into infinite time.

But the minds set on fire by this ideal have not all received an equal share of calm from the creative genius—that great and patient temper which is required to impress the ideal on the dumb marble, or to spread it over a page of cold, sober letters, and then intrust it to the faithful hands of time. This divine instinct, and creative force, much too ardent to follow this peaceful walk, often throws itself immediately on the present, on active life, and strives to transform the shapeless matter of the moral world. The misfortune of his brothers, of the whole species, appeals loudly to the heart of the man of feeling; their abasement appeals still louder: enthusiasm is inflamed, and in souls endowed with energy the burning desire aspires impatiently to action and facts. But has this innovator examined himself to see if these disorders of the moral world wound his reason, or if they do not rather wound his self-love? If he does not determine this point at once, he will find it from the impulsiveness with which he pursues a prompt and definite end. A pure, moral motive has for its end the absolute; time does not exist for it, and the future becomes the present to it directly; by a necessary development, it has to issue from the present. To a reason having no limits the direction towards an end becomes confounded with the accomplishment of this end, and to enter on a course is to have finished it.

If, then, a young friend of the true and of the beautiful were to ask me how, notwithstanding the resistance of the times, he can satisfy the noble longing of his heart, I should reply: Direct the world on which you act towards that which is good, and the measured and peaceful course of time will bring about the results. You have given it this direction if by your teaching you raise its thoughts towards the necessary and the eternal; if, by your acts or your creations, you make the necessary and the eternal the object of your leanings. The structure of error and of all that is arbitrary must fall, and it has already fallen, as soon as you are sure that it is tottering. But it is important that it should not only totter in the external but also in the internal man. Cherish triumphant truth in the modest sanctuary of your heart; give it an incarnate form through beauty, that it may not only be in the understanding that does homage to it, but that feeling may lovingly grasp its appearance. And that you may not by any chance take from

Letters on the Aesthetical Education of Man

external reality the model which you yourself ought to furnish, do not venture into its dangerous society before you are assured in your own heart that you have a good escort furnished by ideal nature. Live with your age, but be not its creation; labor for your contemporaries, but do for them what they need, and not what they praise. Without having shared their faults, share their punishment with a noble resignation, and bend under the yoke which they find it as painful to dispense with as to bear. By the constancy with which you will despise their good fortune, you will prove to them that it is not through cowardice that you submit to their sufferings. See them in thought such as they ought to be when you must act upon them; but see them as they are when you are tempted to act for them. Seek to owe their suffrage to their dignity; but to make them happy keep an account of their unworthiness: thus, on the one hand, the nobleness of your heart will kindle theirs, and, on the other, your end will not be reduced to nothingness by their unworthiness. The gravity of your principles will keep them off from you, but in play they will still endure them. Their taste is purer than their heart, and it is by their taste you must lay hold of this suspicious fugitive. In vain will you combat their maxims, in vain will you condemn their actions; but you can try your moulding hand on their leisure. Drive away caprice, frivolity, and coarseness from their pleasures, and you will banish them imperceptibly from their acts, and at length from their feelings. Everywhere that you meet them, surround them with great, noble, and ingenious forms; multiply around them the symbols of perfection, till appearance triumphs over reality, and art over nature.

Letter X

Convinced by my preceding letters, you agree with me on this point, that man can depart from his destination by two opposite roads, that our epoch is actually moving on these two false roads, and that it has become the prey, in one case, of coarseness, and elsewhere of exhaustion and depravity. It is the beautiful that must bring it back from this twofold departure. But how can the cultivation of the fine arts remedy, at the same time, these opposite defects, and unite in itself two contradictory qualities? Can it bind nature in the savage, and set it free in the barbarian? Can it at once tighten a spring and loose it; and if it cannot produce this double effect, how will it be reasonable to expect from it so important a result as the education of man?

It may be urged that it is almost a proverbial adage that the feeling developed by the beautiful refines manners, and any new proof offered on the subject would appear superfluous. Men base this maxim on daily experience, which shows us almost always clearness of intellect, delicacy of feeling, liberality and even dignity of conduct, associated with a cultivated taste, while an uncultivated taste is almost always accompanied by the opposite qualities. With considerable assurance, the most civilized nation of antiquity is cited as an evidence of this, the Greeks, among whom the perception of the beautiful attained its highest development, and, as a contrast, it is usual to point to nations in a partial savage state, and partly barbarous, who expiate their insensibility to the beautiful by a coarse, or, at all events, a hard, austere character. Nevertheless, some thinkers are tempted occasionally to deny either the fact itself or to dispute the legitimacy of the consequences that are derived from it. They do not entertain so unfavorable an opinion of that savage coarseness which is made a reproach in the case of certain nations; nor do they form so advantageous an opinion of the refinement so highly lauded in the case of cultivated nations. Even as far back as in antiquity there were men who by no means regarded the culture of the liberal arts as a benefit, and who were consequently led to forbid the entrance of their republic to imagination.

I do not speak of those who calumniate art because they have never been favored by it. These persons only appreciate a possession by the trouble it takes to acquire it, and by the profit it brings: and how could they properly appreciate the silent labor of taste in the exterior and interior man? How evident it is that the accidental disadvantages attending liberal culture would make them lose sight of its essential advantages? The man deficient in form despises the grace of diction as a means of corruption, courtesy in the social relations as dissimulation, delicacy and generosity in conduct as an affected exaggeration. He cannot forgive the favorite of the Graces for having enlivened all assemblies as a man of the world, of having directed all men to his views like a statesman, and of giving his impress to the whole century as a writer: while he, the victim of labor, can only obtain with all his learning, the least attention or overcome the least difficulty. As he cannot learn from his fortunate rival the secret of pleasing, the only course open to him is to deplore the corruption of human nature, which adores rather the appearance than the reality.

But there are also opinions deserving respect, that pronounce themselves adverse to the effects of the beautiful, and find formidable arms in experience, with which to wage war against it. "We are free to admit"— such is their language—"that the charms of the beautiful can further honorable ends in pure hands; but it is not repugnant to its nature to produce, in impure hands, a directly contrary effect, and to employ in the service of injustice and error the power that throws the soul of man into chains. It is exactly because taste only attends to the form and never to the substance; it ends by placing the soul on the dangerous incline, leading it to neglect all reality and to sacrifice truth and morality to an attractive envelope. All the real difference of things vanishes, and it is only the appearance that determines the value! How many men of talent"—thus these arguers proceed—"have been turned aside from all effort by the seductive power of the beautiful, or have been led away from all serious exercise of their activity, or have been induced to use it very feebly? How many weak minds have been impelled to quarrel with the organizations of society, simply because it has pleased the imagination of poets to present the image of a world constituted differently, where no propriety chains down opinion and no artifice holds nature in thraldom? What a dangerous logic of the passions they have learned since the poets have painted them in their pictures in the most brilliant colors, and since, in the contest with law and duty, they have commonly remained masters of the battle-field. What has society gained by the relations of society, formerly under the sway of truth, being now subject to the laws of the beautiful, or by the external impression deciding the estimation in which merit is to be held? We admit that all virtues whose appearance produces an agreeable effect are now seen to flourish, and those which, in society, give a value to the man who possesses them. But, as a compensation, all kinds of excesses are seen to prevail, and all vices are in vogue that can be reconciled with a graceful exterior." It is certainly a matter entitled to reflection that, at almost all the periods of history when art flourished and taste held sway, humanity is found in a state of decline; nor can a single instance be cited of the union of a large diffusion of aesthetic culture with political liberty and social virtue, of fine manners associated with good morals, and of politeness fraternizing with truth and loyalty of character and life.

As long as Athens and Sparta preserved their independence, and as long as their institutions were based on respect for the laws, taste did not reach its maturity, art remained in its infancy, and beauty was far from exercising her empire over minds. No doubt, poetry had already taken a sublime flight, but it was on the wings of genius, and we know that genius borders very closely on savage coarseness, that it is a light which shines readily in the midst of darkness, and which therefore often argues against rather than in favor of the taste of time. When the golden age of art appears under Pericles and Alexander, and the sway of taste becomes more general, strength and liberty have abandoned Greece; eloquence corrupts the truth, wisdom offends it on the lips of Socrates, and virtue in the life of Phocion. It is well known that the Romans had to exhaust their energies in civil wars, and, corrupted by Oriental luxury, to bow their heads under the yoke of a fortunate despot, before Grecian art triumphed over the stiffness of their character. The same was the case with the Arabs: civilization only dawned upon them when the vigor of their military spirit became softened under the sceptre of the Abbassides. Art did not appear in modern Italy till the glorious Lombard League was dissolved, Florence submitting to the Medici; and all those brave cities gave up the spirit of independence for an inglorious resignation. It is almost superfluous to call to mind the example of modern nations, with whom refinement has increased in direct proportion to the decline of their liberties. Wherever we direct our eyes in past times, we see taste and freedom mutually avoiding each other. Everywhere we see that the beautiful only founds its sway on the ruins of heroic virtues.

And yet this strength of character, which is commonly sacrificed to establish aesthetic culture, is the most powerful spring of all that is great and excellent in man, and no other advantage, however great, can make up for it. Accordingly, if we only keep to the experiments hitherto made, as to the influence of the beautiful, we cannot certainly be much encouraged in developing feelings so dangerous to the real culture of man. At the risk of being hard and coarse, it will seem preferable to dispense with this dissolving force of the beautiful rather than see human nature a prey to its enervating influence, notwithstanding all its refining advantages. However, experience is perhaps not the proper tribunal at which to decide such a question; before giving so much weight to its testimony, it would be well to inquire if the beauty we have been discussing is the power that is condemned by the previous examples. And the beauty we are discussing seems to assume an idea of the beautiful derived from a source different from experience, for it is this higher notion of the beautiful which has to decide if what is called beauty by experience is entitled to the name.

This pure and rational idea of the beautiful—supposing it can be placed in evidence—cannot be taken from any real and special case, and must, on the contrary, direct and give sanction to our judgment in each special case. It must therefore be sought for by a process of abstraction, and it ought to be deduced from the simple possibility of a nature both sensuous and rational; in short, beauty ought to present itself as a necessary condition of humanity. It is therefore essential that we should rise to the pure idea of humanity, and as experience shows us nothing but individuals, in particular cases, and never humanity at large, we must endeavor to find in their individual and variable mode of being the absolute and the permanent, and to grasp the necessary conditions of their existence, suppressing all accidental limits. No doubt this transcendental procedure will remove us for some time from the familiar circle of phenomena, and the living presence of objects, to keep us on the unproductive ground of abstract idea; but we are engaged in the search after a principle of knowledge solid enough not to be shaken by anything, and the man who does not dare to rise above reality will never conquer this truth.

Letter XI

If abstraction rises to as great an elevation as possible, it arrives at two primary ideas, before which it is obliged to stop and to recognize its limits. It distinguishes in man something that continues, and something that changes incessantly. That which continues it names his person; that which changes his position, his condition.

The person and the condition, I and my determinations, which we represent as one and the same thing in the necessary being, are eternally distinct in the finite being. Notwithstanding all continuance in the person, the condition changes; in spite of all change of condition the person remains. We pass from rest to activity, from emotion to indifference, from assent to contradiction, but we are always *we ourselves*, and what immediately springs from *ourselves* remains. It is only in the absolute subject that all his determinations continue with his personality. All that Divinity is, it is because it is so; consequently it is eternally what it is, because it is eternal.

As the person and the condition are distinct in man, because he is a finite being, the condition cannot be founded on the person, nor the person on the condition. Admitting the second case, the person would have to change; and in the former case, the condition would have to continue. Thus in either supposition, either the personality or the quality of a finite being would necessarily cease. It is not because we think, feel, and will that we are; it is not because we are that we think, feel, and will. We are because we are. We feel, think, and will because there is out of us something that is not ourselves.

Consequently the person must have its principle of existence in itself, because the permanent cannot be derived from the changeable, and thus we should be at once in possession of the idea of the absolute being, founded on itself; that is to say, of the *idea of freedom*. The condition must have a foundation, and as it is not through the person, and is not therefore absolute, it must be a *sequence* and a *result*; and thus, in the second place, we should have arrived at the condition of every independent being, of everything in the process of becoming something else: that is, of the idea of *time*. "Time is the necessary condition of all processes, of becoming (Werden);" this is an identical proposition, for it says nothing but this: "That something may follow, there must be a succession."

The person which manifested itself in the eternally continuing Ego, or I myself, and only in him, cannot become something or begin in time, because it is much rather time that must begin with him, because the permanent must serve as basis to the changeable. That change may take place, something must change; this something cannot therefore be the change itself. When we say the flower opens and fades, we make of this flower a permanent being in the midst of this transformation; we lend it, in some sort, a personality, in which these two conditions are manifested. It cannot be objected that man is born, and becomes something; for man is not only a person simply, but he is a person finding himself in a determinate condition. Now our determinate state of condition springs up in time, and it is thus that man, as a phenomenon or appearance, must have a beginning, though in him pure intelligence is eternal. Without time, that is, without a becoming, he would not be a determinate being; his personality would exist virtually no doubt, but not in action. It is not by the succession of its perceptions that the immutable Ego or person manifests himself to himself.

Thus, therefore, the matter of activity, or reality, that the supreme intelligence draws from its own being, must be *received* by man; and he does, in fact, receive it, through the medium of perception, as something which is outside him in space, and which changes in him in time. This matter which changes in him is always accompanied by the Ego, the personality, that never changes; and the rule prescribed for man by his rational nature is to remain immutably *himself* in the midst of change, to refer all perceptions to experience, that is, to the unity of knowledge, and to make of each of its manifestations of its modes in time the law of all time. The matter only exists in as far as it changes: *he*, his personality, only exists in as far as he does not change. Consequently, represented in his perfection, man would be the permanent unity, which remains always the same, among the waves of change.

Now, although an infinite being, a divinity could not *become* (or be subject to time), still a tendency ought to be named divine which has for its infinite end the most characteristic attribute of the divinity; the absolute manifestation of power—the reality of all the possible—and the absolute unity of the manifestation (the necessity of all reality). It cannot be disputed that man bears within himself, in his personality, a predisposition for divinity. The way to divinity — if the word "way" can be applied to what never leads to its end — is open to him in every *direction*.

Considered in itself, and independently of all sensuous matter, his personality is nothing but the pure virtuality of a possible infinite manifestation; and so long as there is neither intuition nor feeling, it is nothing more than a form, an empty power. Considered in itself, and independently of all spontaneous activity of the mind, sensuousness can only make a material man; without it, it is a pure form; but it cannot in any way establish a union between matter and it. So long as he only feels, wishes, and acts under the influence of desire, he is nothing more than the world, if by this word we point out only the formless contents of time. Without doubt, it is only his sensuousness that makes his strength pass into efficacious acts, but it is his personality alone that makes this activity his own. Thus, that he may not only be a world, he must give form to matter, and in order not to be a mere form, he must give reality to the virtuality that he bears in him. He gives matter to form by creating time, and by opposing the immutable to change, the diversity of the world to the eternal unity of the Ego. He gives a form to matter by again suppressing time, by maintaining permanence in change, and by placing the diversity of the world under the unity of the Ego.

Now from this source issue for man two opposite exigencies, the two fundamental laws of sensuous-rational nature. The first has for its object absolute *reality*; it must make a world of what is only form, manifest all that in it is only a force. The second law has for its object absolute *formality*; it must destroy in him all that is only world, and carry out harmony in all changes. In other terms, he must manifest all that is internal, and give form to all that is external. Considered in its most lofty accomplishment, this twofold labor brings back to the idea of humanity, which was my starting-point.

Letter XII

This twofold labor or task, which consists in making the necessary pass into reality in us and in making *out of us* reality subject to the law of necessity, is urged upon us as a duty by two opposing forces, which are justly styled impulsions or instincts, because they impel us to realize their object. The first of these impulsions, which I shall call the *sensuous instinct*, issues from the physical existence of man, or from sensuous nature; and it is this instinct which tends to enclose him in the limits of time, and to make of him a material being; I do not say to give him matter, for to do that a certain free activity of the personality would be necessary, which, receiving matter, distinguishes it from the Ego, or what is permanent. By matter I only understand in this place the change or reality that fills time. Consequently the instinct requires that there should be change, and that time should contain something. This simply filled state of time is named sensation, and it is only in this state that physical existence manifests itself.

As all that is in time is *successive*, it follows by that fact alone that something is: all the remainder is excluded. When one note on an instrument is touched, among all those that it virtually offers, this note alone is real. When man is actually modified, the infinite possibility of all his modifications is limited to this single mode of existence. Thus, then, the exclusive action of sensuous impulsion has for its necessary consequence the narrowest limitation. In this state man is only a unity of magnitude, a complete moment in time; or, to speak more correctly, *he* is not, for his personality is suppressed as long as sensation holds sway over him and carries time along with it.

This instinct extends its domains over the entire sphere of the finite in man, and as form is only revealed in matter, and the absolute by means of its limits, the total manifestation of human nature is connected on a close analysis with the sensuous instinct. But though it is only this instinct that awakens and develops what exists virtually in man, it is nevertheless this very instinct which renders his perfection impossible. It binds down to the world of sense by indestructible ties the spirit that tends higher, and it calls back to the limits of the present, abstraction which had its free development in the sphere of the infinite. No doubt, thought can escape it for a moment, and a firm will victoriously resist its exigencies: but soon compressed nature resumes her rights to give an imperious reality to our existence, to give it contents, substance, knowledge, and an aim for our activity.

The second impulsion, which may be named the *formal instinct*, issues from the absolute existence of man, or from his rational nature, and tends to set free, and bring harmony into the diversity of its manifestations, and to maintain personality notwithstanding all the changes of state. As this personality, being an absolute and indivisible unity, can never be in contradiction with itself, as *we are ourselves* forever, this impulsion, which tends to maintain personality, can never exact in one time anything but what it exacts and requires

Letters on the Aesthetical Education of Man

forever. It therefore decides for always what it decides now, and orders now what it orders forever. Hence it embraces the whole series of times, or what comes to the same thing, it suppresses time and change. It wishes the real to be necessary and eternal, and it wishes the eternal and the necessary to be real; in other terms, it tends to truth and justice.

If the sensuous instinct only produces *accidents*, the formal instinct gives laws, laws for every judgment when it is a question of knowledge, laws for every will when it is a question of action. Whether, therefore, we recognize an object or conceive an objective value to a state of the subject, whether we act in virtue of knowledge or make of the objective the determining principle of our state; in both cases we withdraw this state from the jurisdiction of time, and we attribute to it reality for all men and for all time, that is, universality and necessity. Feeling can only say: "That is true *for this subject* and *at this moment*," and there may come another moment, another subject, which withdraws the affirmation from the actual feeling. But when once thought pronounces and says: "*That is*," it decides forever and ever, and the validity of its decision is guaranteed by the personality itself, which defies all change. Inclination can only say: "That is good *for your individuality and present necessity*"; but the changing current of affairs will sweep them away, and what you ardently desire to-day will form the object of your aversion to-morrow. But when the moral feeling says: "That ought to be," it decides forever. If you confess the truth because it is the truth, and if you practise justice because it is justice, you have made of a particular case the law of all possible cases, and treated one moment of your life as eternity.

Accordingly, when the formal impulse holds sway and the pure object acts in us, the being attains its highest expansion, all barriers disappear, and from the unity of magnitude in which man was enclosed by a narrow sensuousness, he rises to the *unity of idea*, which embraces and keeps subject the entire sphere of phenomena. During this operation we are no longer in time, but time is in us with its infinite succession. We are no longer individuals but a species; the judgment of all spirits is expressed by our own, and the choice of all hearts is represented by our own act.

Letter XIII

O n a first survey, nothing appears more opposed than these two impulsions; one having for its object change, the other immutability, and yet it is these two notions that exhaust the notion of humanity, and a third *fundamental impulsion*, holding a medium between them, is quite inconceivable. How then shall we re-establish the unity of human nature, a unity that appears completely destroyed by this primitive and radical opposition?

I admit these two tendencies are contradictory, but it should be noticed that they are not so in the *same objects*. But things that do not meet cannot come into collision. No doubt the sensuous impulsion desires change; but it does not wish that it should extend to personality and its field, nor that there should be a change of principles. The formal impulsion seeks unity and permanence, but it does not wish the condition to remain fixed with the person, that there should be identity of feeling. Therefore these two impulsions are not divided by nature, and if, nevertheless, they appear so, it is because they have become divided by transgressing nature freely, by ignoring themselves, and by confounding their spheres. The office of culture is to watch over them and to secure to each one its proper *limits*; therefore culture has to give equal justice to both, and to defend not only the rational impulsion against the sensuous, but also the latter against the former. Hence she has to act a twofold part: first, to protect sense against the attacks of freedom; secondly, to secure personality against the power of sensations. One of these ends is attained by the cultivation of the sensuous, the other by that of reason.

Since the world is developed in time, or change, the perfection of the faculty that places men in relation with the world will necessarily be the greatest possible mutability and extensiveness. Since personality is permanence in change, the perfection of this faculty, which must be opposed to change, will be the greatest possible freedom of action (autonomy) and intensity. The more the receptivity is developed under manifold aspects, the more it is movable and offers surfaces to phenomena, the larger is the part of the world *seized* upon by man, and the more virtualities he develops in himself. Again, in proportion as man gains strength and depth, and depth and reason gain in freedom, in that proportion man *takes in* a larger share of the world, and throws out forms outside himself. Therefore his culture will consist, first, in placing his receptivity in contact with the world in the greatest number of points possible, and in raising passivity, to the highest exponent on the side of feeling; secondly, in procuring for the determining faculty the greatest possible amount of independence, in relation to the receptive power, and in raising activity to the highest degree on the side of reason. By the union of these two qualities man will associate the highest degree of self-spontaneity (autonomy) and of freedom with the fullest plenitude of existence, and instead of abandoning himself to the world so as to get lost in it, he will rather absorb it in himself, with all the infinitude of its phenomena, and subject it to the unity of his reason.

But man can invert this relation, and thus fail in attaining his destination in two ways. He can hand over to the passive force the intensity demanded by the active force; he can encroach by material impulsion on the formal impulsion, and convert the receptive into the determining power. He can attribute to the active force the extensiveness belonging to the passive force, he can encroach by the formal impulsion on the material impulsion, and substitute the determining for the receptive power. In the former case, he will never be an Ego, a personality; in the second case, he will never be a Non-Ego, and hence in both cases he will be *neither the one nor the other*, consequently he will be nothing.

In fact, if the sensuous impulsion becomes determining, if the senses become lawgivers, and if the world stifles personality, he loses as object what he gains in force. It may be said of man that when he is only the contents of time, he is not and consequently *he has* no other contents. His condition is destroyed at the same time as his personality, because these are two correlative ideas, because change presupposes permanence, and a limited reality implies an infinite reality. If the formal impulsion becomes receptive, that is, if thought anticipates sensation, and the person substitutes itself in the place of the world, it loses as a subject and autonomous force what it gains as object, because immutability implies change, and that to manifest itself also absolute reality requires limits. As soon as man is only form, he has no form, and the personality vanishes with the condition. In a word, it is only inasmuch as he is spontaneous, autonomous, that there is reality out of him, that he is also receptive; and it is only inasmuch as he is receptive that there is reality in him, that he is a thinking force.

Consequently these two impulsions require limits, and looked upon as forces, they need tempering; the former that it may not encroach on the field of legislation, the latter that it may not invade the ground of feeling. But this tempering and moderating the sensuous impulsion ought not to be the effect of physical impotence or of a blunting of sensations, which is always a matter for contempt. It must be a free act, an activity of the person, which by its moral intensity moderates the sensuous intensity, and by the sway of impressions takes from them in depth what it gives them in surface or breadth. The character must place limits to temperament, for the senses have only the right to lose elements if it be to the advantage of the mind. In its turn, the tempering of the formal impulsion must not result from moral impotence, from a relaxation of thought and will, which would degrade humanity. It is necessary that the glorious source of this second tempering should be the fulness of sensations; it is necessary that sensuousness itself should defend its field with a victorious arm and resist the violence that the invading activity of the mind would do to it. In a word, it is necessary that the material impulsion should be contained in the limits of propriety by personality, and the formal impulsion by receptivity or nature.

Letter XIV

We have been brought to the idea of such a correlation between the two impulsions that the action of the one establishes and limits at the same time the action of the other, and that each of them, taken in isolation, does arrive at its highest manifestation just because the other is active.

No doubt this correlation of the two impulsions is simply a problem advanced by reason, and which man will only be able to solve in the perfection of his being. It is in the strictest signification of the term: *the idea of his humanity*; accordingly, it is an infinite to which he can approach nearer and nearer in the course of time, but without ever reaching it. "He ought not to aim at form to the injury of reality, nor to reality to the detriment of the form. He must rather seek the absolute being by means of a determinate being, and the determinate being by means of an infinite being. He must set the world before him because he is a person, and he must be a person because he has the world before him. He must feel because he has a consciousness of himself, and he must have a consciousness of himself because he feels." It is only in conformity with this idea that he is a man in the full sense of the word; but he cannot be convinced of this so long as he gives himself up exclusively to one of these two impulsions, or only satisfies them one after the other. For as long as he only feels, his absolute personality and existence remain a mystery to him, and as long as he only thinks, his condition or existence in time escapes him. But if there were cases in which he could have *at once* this twofold experience in which he would have the consciousness of his freedom and the feeling of his existence together, in which he would simultaneously feel as matter and know himself as spirit, in such cases, and in such only, would he have a complete intuition of his humanity, and the object that would procure him this intuition would be a symbol of his accomplished destiny and consequently serve to express the infinite to him—since this destination can only be fulfilled in the fulness of time.

Presuming that cases of this kind could present themselves in experience, they would awake in him a new impulsion, which, precisely because the other two impulsions would co-operate in it, would be opposed to each of them taken in isolation, and might, with good grounds, be taken for a new impulsion. The sensuous impulsion requires that there should be change, that time should have contents; the formal impulsion requires that time should be suppressed, that there should be no change. Consequently, the impulsion in which both of the others act in concert—allow me to call it the *instinct of play*, till I explain the term—the instinct of play would have as its object to suppress time in time, to conciliate the state of transition or *becoming* with the absolute being, change with identity.

The sensuous instinct wishes to be determined, it wishes to receive an object; the formal instinct wishes to determine itself, it wishes to produce an object. Therefore the instinct of play will endeavor to receive as it would itself have produced, and to produce as it aspires to receive.

The sensuous impulsion excludes from its subject all autonomy and freedom; the formal impulsion excludes all dependence and passivity. But the exclusion of freedom is physical necessity; the exclusion of passivity is moral necessity. Thus the two impulsions subdue the mind: the former to the laws of nature, the latter to the laws of reason. It results from this that the instinct of play, which unites the double action of the two other instincts, will content the mind at once morally and physically. Hence, as it suppresses all that is contingent, it will also suppress all coercion, and will set man free physically and morally. When we welcome with effusion some one who deserves our contempt, we feel painfully that *nature is constrained*. When we have a hostile feeling against a person who commands our esteem, we feel painfully the *constraint of reason*. But if this person inspires us with interest, and also wins our esteem, the constraint of feeling vanishes together with the constraint of reason, and we begin to love him, that is to say, to play, to take recreation, at once with our inclination and our esteem.

Moreover, as the sensuous impulsion controls us physically, and the formal impulsion morally, the former makes our formal constitution contingent, and the latter makes our material constitution contingent, that is to say, there is contingence in the agreement of our happiness with our perfection, and reciprocally. The instinct of play, in which both act in concert, will render both our formal and our material constitution contingent; accordingly, our perfection and our happiness in like manner. And on the other hand, exactly because it makes *both of them* contingent, and because the contingent disappears with necessity, it will suppress this contingence in both, and will thus give form to matter and reality to form. In proportion that it will lessen the dynamic influence of feeling and passion, it will place them in harmony with rational ideas, and by taking from the laws of reason their moral constraint, it will reconcile them with the interest of the senses.

Letter XV

I approach continually nearer to the end to which I lead you, by a path offering few attractions. Be pleased to follow me a few steps further, and a large horizon will open up to you, and a delightful prospect will reward you for the labor of the way.

The object of the sensuous instinct, expressed in a universal conception, is named Life in the widest acceptation; a conception that expresses all material existence and all that is immediately present in the senses. The object of the formal instinct, expressed in a universal conception, is called shape or form, as well in an exact as in an inexact acceptation; a conception that embraces all formal qualities of things and all relations of the same to the thinking powers. The object of the play instinct, represented in a general statement, may therefore bear the name of *living form*; a term that serves to describe all aesthetic qualities of phenomena, and what people style, in the widest sense, *beauty*.

Beauty is neither extended to the whole field of all living things nor merely enclosed in this field. A marble block, though it is and remains lifeless, can nevertheless become a living form by the architect and sculptor; a man, though he lives and has a form, is far from being a living form on that account. For this to be the case, it is necessary that his form should be life, and that his life should be a form. As long as we only think of his form, it is lifeless, a mere abstraction; as long as we only feel his life, it is without form, a mere impression. It is only when his form lives in our feeling, and his life in our understanding, he is the living form, and this will everywhere be the case where we judge him to be beautiful.

But the genesis of beauty is by no means declared because we know how to point out the component parts, which in their combination produce beauty. For to this end it would be necessary to comprehend that *combination itself*, which continues to defy our exploration, as well as all mutual operation between the finite and the infinite. The reason, on transcendental grounds, makes the following demand: There shall be a communion between the formal impulse and the material impulse—that is, there shall be a play instinct— because it is only the unity of reality with the form, of the accidental with the necessary, of the passive state with freedom, that the conception of humanity is completed. Reason is obliged to make this demand, because her nature impels her to completeness and to the removal of all bounds; while every exclusive activity of one or the other impulse leaves human nature incomplete and places a limit in it. Accordingly, as soon as reason issues the mandate, "a humanity shall exist," it proclaims at the same time the law, "there shall be a beauty." Experience can answer us if there is a beauty, and we shall know it as soon as she has taught us if a humanity can exist. But neither reason nor experience can tell us how beauty can be and how a humanity is possible.

We know that man is neither exclusively matter nor exclusively spirit. Accordingly, beauty as the consummation of humanity, can neither be exclusively mere life, as has been asserted by sharp-sighted observers, who kept too close to the testimony of experience, and to which the taste of the time would gladly degrade it; Nor can beauty be merely form, as has been judged by speculative sophists, who departed too far from experience, and by philosophic artists, who were led too much by the necessity of art in explaining beauty; it is rather the common object of both impulses, that is of the play instinct. The use of language completely justifies this name, as it is wont to qualify with the word play what is neither subjectively nor objectively accidental, and yet does not impose necessity either externally or internally. As the mind in the intuition of the beautiful finds itself in a happy medium between law and necessity, it is, because it divides itself between both, emancipated from the pressure of both. The formal impulse and the material impulse are equally earnest in their demands, because one relates in its cognition to things in their reality and the other to their necessity; because in action the first is directed to the preservation of life, the second to the preservation of dignity, and therefore both to truth and perfection. But life becomes more indifferent when dignity is mixed up with it, and duty no longer coerces when inclination attracts. In like manner the mind takes in the reality of things, material truth, more freely and tranquilly as soon as it encounters formal truth, the law of necessity; nor does the mind find itself strung by abstraction as soon as immediate intuition can accompany it. In one word, when the mind comes into communion with ideas, all reality loses its serious value because it becomes small; and as it comes in contact with feeling, necessity parts also with its serious value because it is *easy*.

But perhaps the objection has for some time occurred to you, Is not the beautiful degraded by this, that it is made a mere play? and is it not reduced to the level of frivolous objects which have for ages passed under that name? Does it not contradict the conception of the reason and the dignity of beauty, which is nevertheless regarded as an instrument of culture, to confine it to the work of being a mere play? and does it not contradict the empirical conception of play, which can coexist with the exclusion of all taste, to confine it merely to beauty?

But what is meant by a *mere play*, when we know that in all conditions of humanity that very thing is play, and only that is play which makes man complete and develops simultaneously his twofold nature? What you style *limitation*, according to your representation of the matter, according to my views, which I have justified by proofs, I name *enlargement*. Consequently I should have said exactly the reverse: man is serious *only* with the agreeable, with the good, and with the perfect, but he *plays* with beauty. In saying this we must not indeed think of the plays that are in vogue in real life, and which commonly refer only to his material state. But in real life we should also seek in vain for the beauty of which we are here speaking. The actually present beauty is worthy of the really, of the actually present play-impulse; but by the ideal of beauty, which is set up by the reason, an ideal of the play-instinct is also presented, which man ought to have before his eyes in all his plays.

Therefore, no error will ever be incurred if we seek the ideal of beauty on the same road on which we satisfy our play-impulse. We can immediately understand why the ideal form of a Venus, of a Juno, and of an Apollo, is to be sought not at Rome, but in Greece, if we contrast the Greek population, delighting in the bloodless athletic contests of boxing, racing, and intellectual rivalry at Olympia, with the Roman people gloating over the agony of a gladiator. Now the reason pronounces that the beautiful must not only be life and form, but a living form, that is, beauty, inasmuch as it dictates to man the twofold law of absolute formality and absolute reality. Reason also utters the decision that man shall only *play* with beauty, and he *shall only play* with *beauty*.

For, to speak out once for all, man only plays when in the full meaning of the word he is a man, and *he is only completely a man when he plays*. This proposition, which at this moment perhaps appears paradoxical, will receive a great and deep meaning if we have advanced far enough to apply it to the twofold seriousness of duty and of destiny. I promise you that the whole edifice of aesthetic art and the still more difficult art of life will be supported by this principle. But this proposition is only unexpected in science; long ago it lived and worked in art and in the feeling of the Greeks, her most accomplished masters; only they removed to Olympus what ought to have been preserved on earth. Influenced by the truth of this principle, they effaced from the brow of their gods the earnestness and labor which furrow the cheeks of mortals, and also the hollow lust that smoothes the empty face. They set free the ever serene from the chains of every purpose, of every duty, of every care, and they made *indolence* and *indifference* the envied condition of the godlike race; merely human appellations for the freest and highest mind. As well the material pressure of natural laws as the spiritual pressure of moral laws lost itself in its higher idea of necessity, which embraced at the same time both worlds, and out of the union of these two necessities issued true freedom. Inspired by this spirit the Greeks also effaced from the features of their ideal, together with *desire* or *inclination*, all traces of *volition*, or, better still, they made both unrecognizable, because they knew how to wed them both in the closest alliance. It is neither charm, nor is it dignity, which speaks from the glorious face of Juno Ludovici; it is neither of these, for it is both at once. While the female god challenges our veneration, the godlike woman at the same time kindles our love. But while in ecstacy we give ourselves up to the heavenly beauty, the heavenly self-repose awes us back. The whole form rests and dwells in itself—a fully complete creation in itself—and as if she were out of space, without advance or resistance; it shows no force contending with force, no opening through which time could break in. Irresistibly carried away and attracted by her womanly charm, kept off at a distance by her godly dignity, we also find ourselves at length in the state of the greatest repose, and the result is a wonderful impression for which the understanding has no idea and language no name.

Letter XVI

From the antagonism of the two impulsions, and from the association of two opposite principles, we have seen beauty to result, of which the highest ideal must therefore be sought in the most perfect union and equilibrium possible of the reality and of the form. But this equilibrium remains always an idea that reality can never completely reach. In reality, there will always remain a preponderance of one of these elements over the other, and the highest point to which experience can reach will consist in an oscillation between two principles, when sometimes reality and at others form will have the advantage. Ideal beauty is therefore eternally one and indivisible, because there can only be one single equilibrium; on the contrary, experimental beauty will be eternally double, because in the oscillation the equilibrium may be destroyed in two ways — this side and that.

I have called attention in the foregoing letters to a fact that can also be rigorously deduced from the considerations that have engaged our attention to the present point; this fact is that an exciting and also a moderating action may be expected from the beautiful. The *tempering* action is directed to keep within proper limits the sensuous and the formal impulsions;

the *exciting*, to maintain both of them in their full force. But these two modes of action of beauty ought to be completely identified in the idea. The beautiful ought to temper while uniformly exciting the two natures, and it ought also to excite while uniformly moderating them. This result flows at once from the idea of a correlation, in virtue of which the two terms mutually imply each other, and are the reciprocal condition one of the other, a correlation of which the purest product is beauty. But experience does not offer an example of so perfect a correlation. In the field of experience it will always happen more or less that excess on the one side will give rise to deficiency on the other, and deficiency will give birth to excess. It results from this that what in the beau-ideal is only distinct in the idea is different in reality in empirical beauty. The beau-ideal, though simple and indivisible, discloses, when viewed in two different aspects, on the one hand, a property of gentleness and grace, and on the other, an energetic property; in experience there is a gentle and graceful beauty and there is an energetic beauty. It is so, and it will be always so, so long as the absolute is enclosed in the limits of time, and the ideas of reason have to be realized in humanity. For example, the intellectual man has the ideal of virtue, of truth, and of happiness; but the active man will only practise virtues, will only grasp *truths*, and enjoy *happy days*. The business of physical and moral education is to bring back this multiplicity to unity, to put morality in the place of manners, science in the place of knowledge; the business of aesthetic education is to make out of beauties the beautiful.

Energetic beauty can no more preserve a man from a certain residue of savage violence and harshness than graceful beauty can secure him against a certain degree of effeminacy and weakness. As it is the effect of the energetic beauty to elevate the mind in a physical and moral point of view and to augment its momentum, it only too often happens that the resistance of the temperament and of the character diminishes the aptitude to receive impressions, that the delicate part of humanity suffers an oppression which ought only to affect its grosser part, and that this coarse nature participates in an increase of force that ought only to turn to the account of free personality. It is for this reason that, at the periods when we find much strength and abundant sap in humanity, true greatness of thought is seen associated with what is gigantic and extravagant, and the sublimest feeling is found coupled with the most horrible excess of passion. It is also the reason why, in the periods distinguished for regularity and form, nature is as often oppressed as it is governed, as often outraged as it is surpassed. And as the action of gentle and graceful beauty is to relax the mind in the moral sphere as well as the physical, it happens quite as easily that the energy of feelings is extinguished with the violence of desires, and that character shares in the loss of strength which ought only to affect the passions. This is the reason why, in ages assumed to be refined, it is not a rare thing to see gentleness degenerate into effeminacy, politeness into platitude, correctness into empty sterility, liberal ways into arbitrary caprice, ease into frivolity, calm into apathy, and, lastly, a most miserable caricature treads on the heels of the noblest, the most beautiful type of humanity. Gentle and graceful beauty is therefore a want to the man who suffers the constraint of manner and of forms, for he is moved by grandeur and strength long before he becomes sensible to harmony and grace. Energetic beauty is a necessity to the man who is under the indulgent sway of taste, for in his state of refinement he is only too much disposed to make light of the strength that he retained in his state of rude savagism.

I think I have now answered and also cleared up the contradiction commonly met in the judgments of men respecting the influence of the beautiful, and the appreciation of aesthetic culture. This contradiction is explained directly we remember that there are two sorts of experimental beauty, and that on both hands an affirmation is extended to the entire race, when it can only be proved of one of the species. This contradiction disappears the moment we distinguish a twofold want in humanity to which two kinds of beauty correspond. It is therefore probable that both sides would make good their claims if they come to an understanding respecting the kind of beauty and the form of humanity that they have in view.

Consequently in the sequel of my researches I shall adopt the course that nature herself follows with man considered from the point of view of aesthetics, and setting out from the two kinds of beauty, I shall rise to the idea of the genus. I shall examine the effects produced on man by the gentle and graceful beauty when its springs of action are in full play, and also those produced by energetic beauty when they are relaxed. I shall do this to confound these two sorts of beauty in the unity of the beau-ideal, in the same way that the two opposite forms and modes of being of humanity are absorbed in the unity of the ideal man.

Letter XVII

While we were only engaged in deducing the universal idea of beauty from the conception of human nature in general, we had only to consider in the latter the limits established essentially in itself, and inseparable from the notion of the finite. Without attending to the contingent restrictions that human nature may undergo in the real world of phenomena, we have drawn the conception of this nature directly from reason, as a source of every necessity, and the ideal of beauty has been given us at the same time with the ideal of humanity.

But now we are coming down from the region of ideas to the scene of reality, to find man in a *determinate state*, and consequently in limits which are not derived from the pure conception of humanity, but from external circumstances and from an accidental use of his freedom. But, although the limitation of the idea of humanity may be very manifold in the individual, the contents of this idea suffice to teach us that we can only depart from it by *two* opposite roads. For if the perfection of man consist in the harmonious energy of his sensuous and spiritual forces, he can only lack this perfection through the want of harmony and the want of energy. Thus, then, before having received on this point the testimony of experience, reason suffices to assure us that we shall find the real and consequently limited man in a state of tension or relaxation, according as the exclusive activity of isolated forces troubles the harmony of his being, or as the unity of his nature is based on the uniform relaxation of his physical and spiritual forces. These opposite limits are, as we have now to prove, suppressed by the beautiful, which re-establishes harmony in man when excited, and energy in man when relaxed; and which, in this way, in conformity with the nature of the beautiful, restores the state of limitation to an absolute state, and makes of man a whole, complete in himself.

Thus the beautiful by no means belies in reality the idea which we have made of it in speculation; only its action is much less free in it than in the field of theory, where we were able to apply it to the pure conception of humanity. In man, as experience shows him to us, the beautiful finds a matter, already damaged and resisting, which robs him in *ideal* perfection of what it communicates to him of its *individual* mode of being. Accordingly in reality the beautiful will always appear a peculiar and limited species, and not as the pure genus; in excited minds in a state of tension it will lose its freedom and variety; in relaxed minds, it will lose its vivifying force; but we, who have become familiar with the true character of this contradictory phenomenon, cannot be led astray by it. We shall not follow the great crowd of critics, in determining their conception by separate experiences, and to make *them* answerable for the deficiencies which man shows under their influence. We know rather that it is man who transfers the imperfections of his individuality over to them, who stands perpetually in the way of their perfection by his subjective limitation, and lowers their absolute ideal to two limited forms of phenomena.

Letters on the Aesthetical Education of Man

It was advanced that soft beauty is for an unstrung mind, and the energetic beauty for the tightly strung mind. But I apply the term unstrung to a man when he is rather under the pressure of feelings than under the pressure of conceptions. Every *exclusive* sway of one of his two fundamental impulses is for man a state of compulsion and violence, and freedom only exists in the co-operation of his two natures. Accordingly, the man governed preponderately by feelings, or sensuously unstrung, is emancipated and set free by matter. The soft and graceful beauty, to satisfy this twofold problem, must therefore show herself under two aspects—in two distinct forms. First, as a form in repose, she will tone down savage life, and pave the way from feeling to thought. She will, secondly, as a living image, equip the abstract form with sensuous power, and lead back the conception to intuition and law to feeling. The former service she does to the man of nature, the second to the man of art. But because she does not in both cases hold complete sway over her matter, but depends on that which is furnished either by formless nature or unnatural art, she will in both cases bear traces of her origin, and lose herself in one place in material life and in another in mere abstract form.

To be able to arrive at a conception how beauty can become a means to remove this twofold relaxation, we must explore its source in the human mind. Accordingly, make up your mind to dwell a little longer in the region of speculation, in order then to leave it forever, and to advance with securer footing on the ground of experience.

Letter XVIII

By beauty the sensuous man is led to form and to thought; by beauty the spiritual man is brought back to matter and restored to the world of sense.

From this statement it would appear to follow that between matter and form, between passivity and activity, there must be a *middle state*, and that beauty plants us in this state. It actually happens that the greater part of mankind really form this conception of beauty as soon as they begin to reflect on its operations, and all experience seems to point to this conclusion. But, on the other hand, nothing is more unwarrantable and contradictory than such a conception, because the aversion of matter and form, the passive and the active, feeling and thought, is *eternal*, and cannot be mediated in any way. How can we remove this contradiction? Beauty weds the two opposed conditions of feeling and thinking, and yet there is absolutely no medium between them. The former is immediately certain through experience, the other through the reason.

This is the point to which the whole question of beauty leads, and if we succeed in settling this point in a satisfactory way, we have at length found the clue that will conduct us through the whole labyrinth of aesthetics.

But this requires two very different operations, which must necessarily support each other in this inquiry. Beauty, it is said, weds two conditions with one another *which are opposite to each other*, and can never be one. We must start from this opposition; we must grasp and recognize them in their entire purity and strictness, so that both conditions are separated in the most definite manner; otherwise we mix, but we do not unite them. Secondly, it is usual to say, beauty *unites* those two opposed conditions, and therefore removes the opposition. But because both conditions remain eternally opposed to one another, they cannot be united in any other way than by being suppressed. Our second business is therefore to make this connection perfect, to carry them out with such purity and perfection that both conditions disappear entirely in a third one, and no trace of separation remains in the whole; otherwise we segregate, but do not unite. All the disputes that have ever prevailed and still prevail in the philosophical world respecting the conception of beauty have no other origin than their commencing without a sufficiently strict distinction, or that it is not carried out fully to a pure union. Those philosophers who blindly follow their *feeling* in reflecting on this topic can obtain no other *conception* of beauty, because they distinguish nothing separate in the totality of the sensuous impression. Other philosophers, who take the understanding as their exclusive guide, can never obtain a conception of beauty, because they never see anything else in the whole than the parts; and spirit and matter remain eternally separate, even in their most perfect unity. The first fear to suppress beauty *dynamically*, that is, as a working power, if they must separate what is united in the feeling. The others fear to suppress beauty *logically*, that is, as a conception, when they have to hold together what in the understanding is separate. The former wish to think of beauty as it works; the latter wish it to work as it is thought. Both therefore must miss the truth; the former, because they try to follow infinite nature with their limited thinking power; the others, because they wish to limit unlimited nature according to their laws of thought. The first fear to rob beauty of its freedom by a too strict dissection, the others fear to destroy the distinctness of the conception by a too violent union. But the former do not reflect that the freedom in which they very properly place the essence of beauty is not lawlessness, but harmony of laws; not caprice, but the highest internal necessity. The others do not remember that distinctness, which they with equal right demand from beauty, does not consist in the *exclusion of certain realities*, but the *absolute including of all*; that is not therefore limitation but infinitude. We shall avoid the quicksands on which both have made shipwreck if we begin from the two elements in which beauty divides itself before the understanding, but then afterwards rise to a pure aesthetic unity by which it works on feeling, and in which both those conditions completely disappear.

Letter XIX

Two principal and different states of passive and active capacity of being determined [Bestimmbarkeit] can be distinguished in man; in like manner two states of passive and active determination [Bestimmung]. The explanation of this proposition leads us most readily to our end.

The condition of the state of man before destination or direction is given him by the impression of the senses is an unlimited capacity of being determined. The infinite of time and space is given to his imagination for its free use; and, because nothing is settled in this kingdom of the possible, and therefore nothing is excluded from it, this state of absence of determination can be named an *empty infiniteness*, which must not by any means be confounded with an infinite void.

Now it is necessary that his sensuous nature should be modified, and that in the indefinite series of possible determinations one alone should become real. One perception must spring up in it. That which, in the previous state of determinableness, was only an empty potency becomes now an active force, and receives contents; but, at the same time, as an active force it receives a limit, after having been, as a simple power, unlimited. Reality exists now, but the infinite has disappeared. To describe a figure in space, we are obliged to *limit* infinite space; to represent to ourselves a change in time, we are obliged to *divide* the totality of time. Thus we only arrive at reality by limitation, at the positive, at a real *position*, by *negation* or exclusion; to determination, by the suppression of our free determinableness.

But mere exclusion would never beget a reality, nor would a mere sensuous impression ever give birth to a perception, if there were not something from which it was excluded, if by an absolute act of the mind the negation were not referred to something positive, and if opposition did not issue out of non-position. This act of the mind is styled judging or thinking, and the result is named *thought*.

Before we determine a place in space, there is no space for us; but without absolute space we could never determine a place. The same is the case with time. Before we have an instant, there is no time to us: but without infinite time — eternity — we should never have a representation of the instant. Thus, therefore, we can only arrive at the whole by the part, to the unlimited through limitation; but reciprocally we only arrive at the part through the whole, at limitation through the unlimited.

It follows from this, that when it is affirmed of beauty that it mediates for man, the transition from feeling to thought, this must not be understood to mean that beauty can fill up the gap that separates feeling from thought, the passive from the active. This gap is infinite; and, without the interposition of a new and independent faculty, it is impossible for the general to issue from the individual, the necessary from the contingent. Thought is the immediate act of this absolute power, which, I admit, can only be manifested in connection with sensuous impressions, but which in this manifestation depends so little on the sensuous that it reveals itself specially in an opposition to it. The spontaneity or autonomy with which it acts excludes every foreign influence; and it is not in as far as it *helps* thought—which comprehends a manifest contradiction but only in as far as it procures for the intellectual faculties the freedom to manifest themselves in conformity with their proper laws. It does it only because the beautiful can become a means of leading man from matter to form, from feeling to laws, from a limited existence to an absolute existence.

But this assumes that the freedom of the intellectual faculties can be balked, which appears contradictory to the conception of an autonomous power. For a power which only receives the matter of its activity from without can only be hindered in its action by the privation of this matter, and consequently by way of negation; it is therefore a misconception of the nature of the mind to attribute to the sensuous passions the power of oppressing positively the freedom of the mind. Experience does indeed present numerous examples where the rational forces appear compressed in proportion to the violence of the sensuous forces. But instead of deducing this spiritual weakness from the energy of passion, this passionate energy must rather be explained by the weakness of the human mind. For the sense can only have a sway such as this over man when the mind has spontaneously neglected to assert its power.

Yet in trying by these explanations to move one objection, I appear to have exposed myself to another, and I have only saved the autonomy of the mind at the cost of its unity. For how can the mind derive at the same time from itself the principles of inactivity and of activity, if it is not itself divided, and if it is not in opposition with itself?

Here we must remember that we have before us, not the infinite mind, but the finite. The finite mind is that which only becomes active through the passive, only arrives at the absolute through limitation, and only acts and fashions in as far as it receives matter. Accordingly, a mind of this nature must associate with the impulse towards form or the absolute, an impulse towards matter or limitation, conditions without which it could not have the former impulse nor satisfy it. How can two such opposite tendencies exist together in the same being? This is a problem that can no doubt embarrass the metaphysician, but not the transcendental philosopher. The latter does not presume to explain the possibility of things, but he is satisfied with giving a solid basis to the knowledge that makes us understand the possibility of experience. And as experience would be equally impossible without this autonomy in the mind, and without the absolute unity of the mind, it lays down these two conceptions as two conditions of experience equally necessary without troubling itself any more to reconcile them. Moreover, this immanence of two fundamental impulses does not in any degree contradict the absolute unity of the mind, as soon as the mind itself, its *selfhood*, is distinguished from those two motors. No doubt, these two impulses *exist* and *act in it*, but *itself* is neither matter nor form, nor the sensuous nor reason, and this is a point that does not seem always to have occurred to those who only look upon the mind as itself acting when its acts are in harmony with reason, and who declare it passive when its acts contradict reason.

Arrived at its development, each of these two fundamental impulsions tends of necessity and by its nature to satisfy itself; but precisely because each of them has a necessary tendency, and both nevertheless have an opposite tendency, this twofold constraint mutually destroys itself, and the will preserves an entire freedom between them both. It is therefore the will that conducts itself like a power—as the basis of reality—with respect to both these impulses; but neither of them can by itself act as a power with respect to the other. A violent man, by his positive tendency to justice, which never fails in him, is turned away from injustice; nor can a temptation of pleasure, however strong, make a strong character violate its principles. There is in man no other power than his will; and death alone, which destroys man, or some privation of self-consciousness, is the only thing that can rob man of his internal freedom.

An *external* necessity determines our condition, our existence in time, by means of the sensuous. The latter is quite involuntary, and directly it is produced in us we are necessarily passive. In the same manner an *internal* necessity awakens our personality in connection with sensations, and by its antagonism with them; for consciousness cannot depend on the will, which presupposes it. This primitive manifestation of personality is no more a merit to us than its privation is a defect in us. Reason can only be required in a being who is self-conscious, for reason is an absolute consecutiveness and universality of consciousness; before this is the case he is not a man, nor can any act of humanity be expected from him. The *metaphysician* can no more explain the limitation imposed by sensation on a free and autonomous mind than the *natural philosopher* can understand the infinite, which is revealed in consciousness in connection with these limits. Neither abstraction nor experience can bring us back to the source whence issue our ideas of necessity and of universality: this source is concealed in its origin in time from the observer, and its super-sensuous origin from the researches of the metaphysician. But, to sum up in a few words, consciousness is there, and, together with its immutable unity, the law of all that *is* for man is established, as well as of all that is to be by man, for his understanding and his activity. The ideas of truth and of right present themselves inevitable, incorruptible, immeasurable, even in the age of sensuousness; and without our being able to say why or how, we see eternity in time, the necessary following the contingent. It is thus that, without any share on the part of the subject, the sensation and self-consciousness arise, and the origin of both is beyond our volition, as it is out of the sphere of our knowledge.

But as soon as these two faculties have passed into action, and man has verified by his experience, through the medium of sensation, a determinate existence, and through the medium of consciousness its absolute existence, the two fundamental impulses exert their influence directly their object is given. The sensuous impulse is awakened with the experience of life—with the beginning of the individual; the rational impulsion with the experience of law—with the beginning of his personality; and it is only when these two inclinations have come into existence that the human type is realized. Up to that time, everything takes place in man according to the law of necessity; but now the hand of *nature* lets him go, and it is for *him* to keep upright humanity, which nature places as a germ in his heart. And thus we see that directly the two opposite and fundamental impulses exercise their influence in him, both lose their constraint, and the autonomy of two necessities gives birth to freedom.

Letter XX

That freedom is an active and not a passive principle results from its very conception; but that liberty itself should be an effect of nature (taking this word in its widest sense), and not the work of man, and therefore that it can be favored or thwarted by natural means, is the necessary consequence of that which precedes. It begins only when man is complete, and when these two fundamental impulsions have been developed. It will then be wanting whilst he is incomplete, and while one of these impulsions is excluded, and it will be re-established by all that gives back to man his integrity.

Thus it is possible, both with regard to the entire species as to the individual, to remark the moment when man is yet incomplete, and when one of the two exclusions acts solely in him. We know that man commences by life simply, to end by form; that he is more of an individual than a person, and that he starts from the limited or finite to approach the infinite. The sensuous impulsion comes into play therefore before the rational impulsion, because sensation precedes consciousness; and in this priority of sensuous impulsion we find the key of the history of the whole of human liberty.

There is a moment, in fact, when the instinct of life, not yet opposed to the instinct of form, acts as nature and as necessity; when the sensuous is a power because man has not begun; for even in man there can be no other power than his will. But when man shall have attained to the power of thought, reason, on the contrary, will be a power, and moral or logical necessity will take the place of physical necessity. Sensuous power must then be annihilated before the law which must govern it can be established. It is not enough that something shall begin which as yet was not; previously something must end which had begun. Man cannot pass immediately from sensuousness to thought. He must step backwards, for it is only when one determination is suppressed that the contrary determination can take place. Consequently, in order to exchange passive against active liberty, a passive determination against an active, he must be momentarily free from all determination, and must traverse a state of pure determinability. He has then to return in some degree to that state of pure negative indetermination in which he was before his senses were affected by anything. But this state was absolutely empty of all contents, and now the question is to reconcile an equal determination and a determinability equally without limit, with the greatest possible fulness, because from this situation something positive must immediately follow. The determination which man received by sensation must be preserved, because he should not lose the reality; but at the same time, in so far as finite, it should be suppressed, because a determinability without limit would take place. The problem consists then in annihilating the determination of the mode of existence, and yet at the same time in preserving it, which is only possible in one way: in *opposing to it another*. The two sides of a balance are in equilibrium when empty; they are also in equilibrium when their contents are of equal weight.

Thus, to pass from sensation to thought, the soul traverses a medium position, in which sensibility and reason are at the same time active, and thus they mutually destroy their determinant power, and by their antagonism produce a negation. This medium situation in which the soul is neither physically nor morally constrained, and yet is in both ways active, merits essentially the name of a free situation; and if we call the state of sensuous determination *physical*, and the state of rational determination *logical or moral*, that state of real and active determination should be called the *aesthetic*.

Letter XXI

I have remarked in the beginning of the foregoing letter that there is a twofold condition of determinableness and a twofold condition of determination. And now I can clear up this proposition.

The mind can be determined — is determinable — only in as far as it is not determined; it is, however, determinable also, in as far as it is not exclusively determined; that is, if it is not confined in its determination. The former is only a want of determination — it is without limits, because it is without reality; but the latter, the aesthetic determinableness, has no limits, because it unites all reality.

The mind is determined, inasmuch as it is only limited; but it is also determined because it limits itself of its own absolute capacity. It is situated in the former position when it feels, in the second when it thinks. Accordingly the aesthetic constitution is in relation to determinableness what thought is in relation to determination. The latter is a negative from internal and infinite completeness, the former a limitation from internal infinite power. Feeling and thought come into contact in one single point, the mind is determined in both conditions, the man becomes something and exists — either as individual or person—by exclusion; in other cases these two faculties stand infinitely apart. Just in the same manner the aesthetic determinableness comes in contact with the mere want of determination in a single point, by both excluding every distinct determined existence, by thus being in all other points nothing and all, and hence by being infinitely different. Therefore if the latter, in the absence of determination from deficiency, is represented as an *empty infiniteness*, the aesthetic freedom of determination, which forms the proper counterpart to the former, can be considered as a *completed infiniteness*; a representation which exactly agrees with the teachings of the previous investigations.

Man is therefore *nothing* in the aesthetic state, if attention is given to the single result, and not to the whole faculty, and if we regard only the absence or want of every special determination. We must therefore do justice to those who pronounce the beautiful, and the disposition in which it places the mind, as entirely indifferent and unprofitable, in relation to *knowledge* and *feeling*. They are perfectly right; for it is certain that beauty gives no separate, single result, either for the understanding or for the will; it does not carry out a single intellectual or moral object; it discovers no truth, does not help us to fulfil a single duty, and, in *one* word, is equally unfit to found the character or to clear the head. Accordingly, the personal worth of a man, or his dignity, as far as this can only depend on himself, remains entirely undetermined by aesthetic culture, and nothing further is attained than that, on the *part of nature*, it is made profitable for him to make of himself what he will; that the freedom to be what he ought to be is restored perfectly to him.

But by this something infinite is attained. But as soon as we remember that freedom is taken from man by the one-sided compulsion of nature in feeling, and by the exclusive legislation of the reason in thinking, we must consider the capacity restored to him by the aesthetical disposition, as the highest of all gifts, as the gift of humanity. I admit that he possesses this capacity for humanity, before every definite determination in which he may be placed. But, as a matter of fact, he loses it with every determined condition into which he may come; and if he is to pass over to an opposite condition, humanity must be in every case restored to him by the aesthetic life.

It is therefore not only a poetical license, but also philosophically correct, when beauty is named our second creator. Nor is this inconsistent with the fact that she only makes it possible for us to attain and realize humanity, leaving this to our free will. For in this she acts in common with our original creator, nature, which has imparted to us nothing further than this capacity for humanity, but leaves the use of it to our own determination of will.

Letters on the Aesthetical Education of Man

Letter XXII

Accordingly, if the aesthetic disposition of the mind must be looked upon in *one* respect as *nothing*—that is, when we confine our view to separate and determined operations—it must be looked upon in another respect as a state of the highest reality, in as far as we attend to the absence of all limits and the sum of powers which are commonly active in it. Accordingly we cannot pronounce them, again, to be wrong who describe the aesthetic state to be the most productive in relation to knowledge and morality. They are perfectly right, for a state of mind which comprises the whole of humanity in itself must of necessity include in itself also —necessarily and potentially—every separate expression of it. Again, a disposition of mind that removes all limitation from the totality of human nature must also remove it from every special expression of the same. Exactly because its "aesthetic disposition" does not exclusively shelter any separate function of humanity, it is favorable to all without distinction; nor does it favor any particular functions, precisely because it is the foundation of the possibility of all. All other exercises give to the mind some special aptitude, but for that very reason give it some definite limits; only the aesthetical leads him to the unlimited. Every other condition in which we can live refers us to a previous condition, and requires for its solution a following condition; only the aesthetic is a complete whole in itself, for it unites in itself all conditions of its source and of its duration. Here alone we feel ourselves swept out of time, and our humanity expresses itself with purity and *integrity* as if it had not yet received any impression or interruption from the operation of external powers.

That which flatters our senses in immediate sensation opens our weak and volatile spirit to every impression, but makes us in the same degree less apt for exertion. That which stretches our thinking power and invites to abstract conceptions strengthens our mind for every kind of resistance, but hardens it also in the same proportion, and deprives us of susceptibility in the same ratio that it helps us to greater mental activity. For this very reason, one as well as the other brings us at length to exhaustion, because matter cannot long do without the shaping, constructive force, and the force cannot do without the constructible material. But on the other hand, if we have resigned ourselves to the enjoyment of genuine beauty, we are at such a moment of our passive and active powers in the same degree master, and we shall turn with ease from grave to gay, from rest to movement, from submission to resistance, to abstract thinking and intuition.

This high indifference and freedom of mind, united with power and elasticity, is the disposition in which a true work of art ought to dismiss us, and there is no better test of true aesthetic excellence. If after an enjoyment of this kind we find ourselves specially impelled to a particular mode of feeling or action, and unfit for other modes, this serves as an infallible proof that we have not experienced *any pure aesthetic* effect, whether this is owing to the object, to our own mode of feeling—as generally happens—or to both together.

As in reality no purely aesthetical effect can be met with—for man can never leave his dependence on material forces—the excellence of a work of art can only consist in its greater approximation to its ideal of aesthetic purity, and however high we may raise the freedom of this effect, we shall always leave it with a particular disposition and a particular bias. Any class of productions or separate work in the world of art is noble and excellent in proportion to the universality of the disposition and the unlimited character of the bias thereby presented to our mind. This truth can be applied to works in various branches of art, and also to different works in the same branch. We leave a grand musical performance with our feelings excited, the reading of a noble poem with a quickened imagination, a beautiful statue or building with an awakened understanding; but a man would not choose an opportune moment who attempted to invite us to abstract thinking after a high musical enjoyment, or to attend to a prosaic affair of common life after a high poetical enjoyment, or to kindle our imagination and astonish our feelings directly after inspecting a fine statue or edifice. The reason of this is, that music, *by its matter*, even when most spiritual, presents a greater affinity with the senses than is permitted by aesthetic liberty; it is because even the most happy poetry, having *for its medium* the arbitrary and contingent play of the imagination, always shares in it more than the intimate necessity of the really beautiful allows; it is because the best sculpture touches on severe science *by what is determinate in its conception.* However, these particular affinities are lost in proportion as the works of these three kinds of art rise to a greater elevation, and it is a natural and necessary consequence of their perfection, that, without confounding their objective limits, the different arts come to resemble each other more and more, in the action *which they exercise on the .mind*. At its highest degree of ennobling, music ought to become a form, and act on us with the calm power of an antique statue; in its most elevated perfection, the plastic art ought to become music and move us by the immediate action exercised on the mind by the senses; in its most complete development, poetry ought both to stir us powerfully like music and like plastic art to surround us with a peaceful light. In each art, the perfect style consists exactly in knowing how to remove specific limits, while sacrificing at the same time the particular advantages of the art, and to give it by a wise use of what belongs to it specially a more general character.

Nor is it only the limits inherent in the specific character of each kind of art that the artist ought to overstep in putting his hand to the work; he must also triumph over those which are inherent in the particular subject of which he treats. In a really beautiful work of art, the substance ought to be inoperative, the form should do everything; for by the form the whole man is acted on; the substance acts on nothing but isolated forces. Thus, however vast and sublime it may be, the substance always exercises a restrictive action on the mind, and true aesthetic liberty can only be expected from the form. Consequently the true search of the matter consists in *destroying matter by the form*; and the triumph of art is great in proportion as it overcomes matter and maintains its sway over those who enjoy its work. It is great particularly in destroying matter when most imposing, ambitious, and attractive, when therefore matter has most power to produce the effect proper to it, or, again, when it leads those who consider it more closely to enter directly into relation with it. The mind of the spectator and of the hearer must remain perfectly free and intact; it must issue pure and entire from the magic circle of the artist, as from the hands of the Creator. The most frivolous subject ought to be treated in such a way that we preserve the faculty to exchange it immediately for the most serious work. The arts which have passion for their object, as a tragedy for example, do not present a difficulty here; for, in the first place, these arts are not entirely free, because they are in the service of a particular end (the pathetic), and then no connoisseur will deny that even in this class a work is perfect in proportion as amidst the most violent storms of passion it respects the liberty of the soul. There is a fine art of passion, but an impassioned fine art is a contradiction in terms, for the infallible effect of the beautiful is emancipation from the passions. The idea of an instructive fine art (didactic art) or improving (moral) art is no less contradictory, for nothing agrees less with the idea of the beautiful than to give a determinate tendency to the mind.

However, from the fact that a work produces effects only by its substance, it must not always be inferred that there is a want of form in this work; this conclusion may quite as well testify to a want of form in the observer. If his mind is too stretched or too relaxed, if it is only accustomed to receive things either by the senses or the intelligence, even in the most perfect combination, it will only stop to look at the parts, and it will only see matter in the most beautiful form. Only sensible of the coarse *elements*, he must first destroy the aesthetic organization of a work to find enjoyment in it, and carefully disinter the details which genius has caused to vanish, with infinite art, in the harmony of the whole. The interest he takes in the work is either solely moral or exclusively physical; the only thing wanting to it is to be exactly what it ought to be—aesthetical. The readers of this class enjoy a serious and pathetic poem as they do a sermon: a simple and playful work, as an inebriating draught; and if on the one hand they have so little taste as to demand *edification* from a tragedy or from an epos, even such as the "Messias," on the other hand they will be infallibly scandalized by a piece after the fashion of Anacreon and Catullus.

Letter XXIII

I take up the thread of my researches, which I broke off only to apply the principles I laid down to practical art and the appreciation of its works.

The transition from the passivity of sensuousness to the activity of thought and of will can be effected only by the intermediary state of aesthetic liberty; and though in itself this state decides nothing respecting our opinions and our sentiments, and therefore it leaves our intellectual and moral value entirely problematical, it is, however, the necessary condition without which we should never attain to an opinion or a sentiment. In a word, there is no other way to make a reasonable being out of a sensuous man than by making him first aesthetic.

But, you might object: Is this mediation absolutely indispensable? Could not truth and duty, one or the other, in themselves and by themselves, find access to the sensuous man? To this I reply: Not only is it possible but it is absolutely necessary that they owe solely to themselves their determining force, and nothing would be more contradictory to our preceding affirmations than to appear to defend the contrary opinion. It has been expressly proved that the beautiful furnishes no result, either for the comprehension or for the will; that it mingles with no operations, either of thought or of resolution; and that it confers this double power without determining anything with regard to the real exercise of this power. Here all foreign help disappears, and the pure logical form, the idea, would speak immediately to the intelligence, as the pure moral form, the law, immediately to the will.

But that the pure form should be capable of it, and that there is in general a pure form for sensuous man, is that, I maintain, which should be rendered possible by the aesthetic disposition of the soul. Truth is not a thing which can be received from without like reality or the visible existence of objects. It is the thinking force, in his own liberty and activity, which produces it, and it is just this liberty proper to it, this liberty which we seek in vain in sensuous man. The sensuous man is already determined physically, and thenceforth he has no longer his free determinability; he must necessarily first enter into possession of this lost determinability before he can exchange the passive against an active determination. Therefore, in order to recover it, he must either lose the passive determination that he had, or he should enclose already in himself the active determination to which he should pass. If he confined himself to lose passive determination, he would at the same time lose with it the possibility of an active determination, because thought needs a body, and form can only be realized through matter. He must therefore contain already in himself the active determination, that he may be at once both actively and passively determined, that is to say, he becomes necessarily aesthetic.

Consequently, by the aesthetic disposition of the soul the proper activity of reason is already revealed in the sphere of sensuousness, the power of sense is already broken within its own boundaries, and the ennobling of physical man carried far enough, for spiritual man has only to develop himself according to the laws of liberty. The transition from an aesthetic state to a logical and moral state (from the beautiful to truth and duty) is then infinitely more easy than the transition from the physical state to the aesthetic state (from life pure and blind to form). This transition man can effectuate alone by his liberty, whilst he has only to enter into possession of himself not to give it himself; but to separate the elements of his nature, and not to enlarge it. Having attained to the aesthetic disposition, man will give to his judgments and to his actions a universal value as soon as he desires it. This passage from brute nature to beauty, in which an entirely new faculty would awaken in him, nature would render easier, and his will has no power over a disposition which, we know, itself gives birth to the will. To bring the aesthetic man to profound views, to elevated sentiments, he requires nothing more than important occasions: to obtain the same thing from the sensuous man, his nature must at first be changed. To make of the former a hero, a sage, it is often only necessary to meet with a sublime situation, which exercises upon the faculty of the will the more immediate action; for the second, it must first be transplanted under another sky.

One of the most important tasks of culture, then, is to submit man to form, even in a purely physical life, and to render it aesthetic as far as the domain of the beautiful can be extended, for it is alone in the aesthetic state, and not in the physical state, that the moral state can be developed. If in each particular case man ought to possess the power to make his judgment and his will the judgment of the entire species; if he ought to find in each limited existence the transition to an infinite existence; if, lastly, he ought from every dependent situation to take his flight to rise to autonomy and to liberty, it must be observed that at no moment he is only individual and solely obeys the laws of nature. To be apt and ready to raise himself from the narrow circle of the ends of nature, to rational ends, in the sphere of the former he must already have exercised himself in the second; he must already have realized his physical destiny with a certain liberty that belongs only to spiritual nature, that is to say according to the laws of the beautiful.

And that he can effect without thwarting in the least degree his physical aim. The exigencies of nature with regard to him turn only upon what he does — upon the substance of his acts; but the ends of nature in no degree determine the way in which he acts, the form of his actions. On the contrary, the exigencies of reason have rigorously the form of his activity for its object. Thus, so much as it is necessary for the moral destination of man, that he be purely moral, that he shows an absolute personal activity, so much is he indifferent that his physical destination be entirely physical, that he acts in a manner entirely passive. Henceforth with regard to this last destination, it entirely depends on him to fulfil it solely as a sensuous being and natural force (as a force which acts only as it diminishes) or, at the same time, as absolute force, as a rational being. To which of these does his dignity best respond? Of this there can be no question. It is as disgraceful and contemptible for him to do under sensuous impulsion that which he ought to have determined merely by the motive of duty, as it is noble and honorable for him to incline towards conformity with laws, harmony, independence; there even where the vulgar man only satisfies a legitimate want. In a word, in the domain of truth and morality, sensuousness must have nothing to determine; but in the sphere of happiness, form may find a place, and the instinct of play prevail.

Thus then, in the indifferent sphere of physical life, man ought to already commence his moral life; his own proper activity ought already to make way in passivity, and his rational liberty beyond the limits of sense; he ought already to impose the law of his will upon his inclinations; he ought—if you will permit me the expression—to carry into the domain of matter the war against matter, in order to be dispensed from combating this redoubtable enemy upon the sacred field of liberty; he ought to learn to have nobler desires, not to be forced to have sublime volitions. This is the fruit of aesthetic culture, which submits to the laws of the beautiful, in which neither the laws of nature nor those of reason suffer, which does not force the will of man, and which by the form it gives to exterior life already opens internal life.

Letter XXIV

Accordingly three different moments or stages of development can be distinguished, which the individual man, as well as the whole race, must of necessity traverse in a determinate order if they are to fulfil the circle of their determination. No doubt, the separate periods can be lengthened or shortened, through accidental causes which are inherent either in the influence of external things or under the free caprice of men: but neither of them can be overstepped, and the order of their sequence cannot be inverted either by nature or by the will. Man, in his physical condition, suffers only the power of nature; he gets rid of this power in the aesthetical condition, and he rules them in the moral state.

What is man before beauty liberates him from free pleasure, and the serenity of form tames down the savageness of life? Eternally uniform in his aims, eternally changing in his judgments, self-seeking without being himself, unfettered without being free, a slave without serving any rule. At this period, the world is to him only destiny, not yet an object; all has existence for him only in as far as it procures existence to him; a thing that neither seeks from nor gives to him is non-existent. Every phenomenon stands out before him separate and cut off, as he finds himself in the series of beings. All that is, is to him through the bias of the moment; every change is to him an entirely fresh creation, because with the necessary *in him*, the necessary *out of him* is wanting, which binds together all the changing forms in the universe, and which holds fast the law on the theatre of his action, while the individual departs. It is in vain that nature lets the rich variety of her forms pass before him; he sees in her glorious fulness nothing but his prey, in her power and greatness nothing but his enemy. Either he encounters objects, and wishes to draw them to himself in desire, or the objects press in a destructive manner upon him, and he thrusts them away in dismay and terror. In both cases his relation to the world of sense is immediate *contact*; and perpetually anxious through its pressure, restless and plagued by imperious wants, he nowhere finds rest except in enervation, and nowhere limits save in exhausted desire.

> "True, his is the powerful breast, and the mighty hand of the Titans. . . .
> A certain inheritance; yet the god welded
> Round his forehead a brazen band;
> Advice, moderation, wisdom, and patience, —
> Hid it from his shy, sinister look.
> Every desire is with him a rage,
> And his rage prowls around limitless." — *Iphigenia in Tauris.*

Ignorant of his own human dignity, he is far removed from honoring it in others, and conscious of his own savage greed, he fears it in every creature that he sees like himself. He never sees others in himself, only himself in others, and human society, instead of enlarging him to the race, only shuts him up continually closer in his individuality. Thus limited, he wanders through his sunless life, till favoring nature rolls away the load of matter from his darkened senses, reflection separates him from things, and objects show themselves at length in the afterglow of the consciousness.

It is true we cannot point out this state of rude nature as we have here portrayed it in any definite people and age. It is only an idea, but an idea with which experience agrees most closely in special features. It may be said that man was never in this animal condition, but he has not, on the other hand, ever entirely escaped from it. Even in the rudest subjects, unmistakable traces of rational freedom can be found, and even in the most cultivated, features are not wanting that remind us of that dismal natural condition. It is possible for man, at one and the same time, to unite the highest and the lowest in his nature; and if his *dignity* depends on a strict separation of one from the other, his *happiness* depends on a skilful removal of this separation. The culture which is to bring his dignity into agreement with his happiness will therefore have to provide for the greatest purity of these two principles in their most intimate combination.

Consequently the first appearance of reason in man is not the beginning of humanity. This is first decided by his freedom, and reason begins first by making his sensuous dependence boundless; a phenomenon that does not appear to me to have been sufficiently elucidated, considering its importance and universality. We know that the reason makes itself known to man by the demand for the absolute—the self-dependent and necessary. But as this want of the reason cannot be satisfied in any separate or single state of his physical life, he is obliged to leave the physical entirely and to rise from a limited reality to ideas. But although the true meaning of that demand of the reason is to withdraw him from the limits of time and to lead him from the world of sense to an ideal world, yet this same demand of reason, by misapplication—scarcely to be avoided in this life, prone to sensuousness—can direct him to physical life, and, instead of making man free, plunge him in the most terrible slavery.

Facts verify this supposition. Man raised on the wings of imagination leaves the narrow limits of the present, in which mere animality is enclosed, in order to strive on to an unlimited future. But while the limitless is unfolded to his dazed *imagination*, his heart has not ceased to live in the separate, and to serve the moment. The impulse towards the absolute seizes him suddenly in the midst of his animality, and as in this cloddish condition all his efforts aim only at the material and temporal, and are limited by his individuality, he is only led by that demand of the reason to extend his individuality into the infinite, instead of to abstract from it. He will be led to seek instead of form an inexhaustible matter, instead of the unchangeable an everlasting change and an absolute securing of his temporal existence. The same impulse which, directed to his thought and action, ought to lead to truth and morality, now directed to his passion and emotional state, produces nothing but an unlimited desire and an absolute want. The first fruits, therefore, that he reaps in the world of spirits are cares and fear—both operations of the reason; not of sensuousness, but of a reason that mistakes its object and applies its categorical imperative to matter. All unconditional systems of happiness are fruits of this tree, whether they have for their object the present day or the whole of life, or what does not make them any more respectable, the whole of eternity, for their object. An unlimited duration of existence and of well-being is only an ideal of the desires; hence a demand which can only be put forth by an animality striving up to the absolute. Man, therefore, without gaining anything for his humanity by a rational expression of this sort, loses the happy limitation of the animal, over which he now only possesses the unenviable superiority of losing the present for an endeavor after what is remote, yet without seeking in the limitless future anything but the present.

But even if the reason does not go astray in its object, or err in the question, sensuousness will continue to falsify the answer for a long time. As soon as man has begun to use his understanding and to knit together phenomena in cause and effect, the reason, according to its conception, presses on to an absolute knitting together and to an unconditional basis. In order, merely, to be able to put forward this demand, man must already have stepped beyond the sensuous, but the sensuous uses this very demand to bring back the fugitive.

In fact, it is now that he ought to abandon entirely the world of sense in order to take his flight into the realm of ideas; for the intelligence remains eternally shut up in the finite and in the contingent, and does not cease putting questions without reaching the last link of the chain. But as the man with whom we are engaged is not yet capable of such an abstraction, and does not find it in the sphere of sensuous knowledge, and because he does not look for it in pure reason, he will seek for it below in the region of sentiment, and will appear to find it. No doubt the sensuous shows him nothing that has its foundation in itself, and that legislates for itself, but it shows him something that does not care for foundation or law; therefore, thus not being able to quiet the intelligence by showing it a final cause, he reduces it to silence by the conception which desires no cause; and being incapable of understanding the sublime necessity of reason, he keeps to the blind constraint of matter. As sensuousness knows no other end than its interest, and is determined by nothing except blind chance, it makes the former the motive of its actions, and the latter the master of the world.

Even the divine part in man, the moral law, in its first manifestation in the sensuous cannot avoid this perversion.

As this moral law is only prohibited, and combats in man the interest of sensuous egotism, it must appear to him as something strange until he has come to consider this self-love as the stranger, and the voice of reason as his true self. Therefore he confines himself to feeling the fetters which the latter imposes on him, without having the consciousness of the infinite emancipation which it procures for him. Without suspecting in himself the dignity of lawgiver, he only experiences the constraint and the impotent revolt of a subject fretting under the yoke, because in this experience the sensuous impulsion precedes the moral impulsion, he gives to the law of necessity a beginning in him, a positive origin, and by the most unfortunate of all mistakes he converts the immutable and the eternal in himself into a transitory accident. He makes up his mind to consider the notions of the just and the unjust as statutes which have been introduced by a will, and not as having in themselves an eternal value. Just as in the explanation of certain natural phenomena he goes beyond nature and seeks out of her what can only be found in her, in her own laws; so also in the explanation of moral phenomena he goes beyond reason and makes light of his humanity, seeking a god in this way. It is not wonderful that a religion which he has purchased at the cost of his humanity shows itself worthy of this origin, and that he only considers as absolute and eternally binding laws that have never been binding from all eternity. He has placed himself in relation with, not a holy being, but a powerful. Therefore the spirit of his religion, of the homage that he gives to God, is a fear that abases him, and not a veneration that elevates him in his own esteem.

Though these different aberrations by which man departs from the ideal of his destination cannot all take place at the same time, because several degrees have to be passed over in the transition from the obscure of thought to error, and from the obscure of will to the corruption of the will; these degrees are all, without exception, the consequence of his physical state, because in all the vital impulsion sways the formal impulsion. Now, two cases may happen: either reason may not yet have spoken in man, and the physical may reign over him with a blind necessity, or reason may not be sufficiently purified from sensuous impressions, and the moral may still be subject to the physical; in both cases the only principle that has a real power over him is a material principle, and man, at least as regards his ultimate tendency, is a sensuous being. The only difference is, that in the former case he is an animal without reason, and in the second case a rational animal. But he ought to be neither one nor the other: he ought to be a man. Nature ought not to rule him exclusively; nor reason conditionally. The two legislations ought to be completely independent, and yet mutually complementary.

Letter XXV

Whilst man, in his first physical condition, is only passively affected by the world of sense, he is still entirely identified with it; and for this reason the external world, as yet, has no objective existence for him. When he begins in his aesthetic state of mind to regard the world objectively, then only is his personality severed from it, and the world appears to him an objective reality, for the simple reason that he has ceased to form an identical portion of it.

That which first connects man with the surrounding universe is the power of reflective contemplation. Whereas desire seizes at once its object, reflection removes it to a distance and renders it inalienably her own by saving it from the greed of passion. The necessity of sense which he obeyed during the period of mere sensations, lessens during the period of reflection; the senses are for the time in abeyance; even ever-fleeting time stands still whilst the scattered rays of consciousness are gathering and shape themselves; an image of the infinite is reflected upon the perishable ground. As soon as light dawns in man, there is no, longer night outside of him; as soon as there is peace within him the storm lulls throughout the universe, and the contending forces of nature find rest within prescribed limits. Hence we cannot wonder if ancient traditions allude to these great changes in the inner man as to a revolution in surrounding nature, and symbolize thought triumphing over the laws of time, by the figure of Zeus, which terminates the reign of Saturn.

As long as man derives sensations from a contact with nature, he is her slave; but as soon as he begins to reflect upon her objects and laws he becomes her lawgiver. Nature, which previously ruled him as a power, now expands before him as an object. What is objective to him can have no power over him, for in order to become objective it has to experience his own power. As far and as long as he impresses a form upon matter, he cannot be injured by its effect; for a spirit can only be injured by that which deprives it of its freedom. Whereas he proves his own freedom by giving a form to the formless; where the mass rules heavily and without shape, and its undefined outlines are for ever fluctuating between uncertain boundaries, fear takes up its abode; but man rises above any natural terror as soon as he knows how to mould it, and transform it into an object of his art. As soon as he upholds his independence towards phenomenal natures he maintains his dignity toward her as a thing of power, and with a noble freedom he rises against his gods. They throw aside the mask with which they had kept him in awe during his infancy, and to his surprise his mind perceives the reflection of his own image. The divine monster of the Oriental, which roams about changing the world with the blind force of a beast of prey, dwindles to the charming outline of humanity in Greek fable; the empire of the Titans is crushed, and boundless force is tamed by infinite form.

But whilst I have been merely searching for an issue from the material world, and a passage into the world of mind, the bold flight of my imagination has already taken me into the very midst of the latter world. The beauty of which we are in search we have left behind by passing from the life of mere sensations to the pure form and to the pure object. Such a leap exceeds the condition of human nature; in order to keep pace with the latter we must return to the world of sense.

Beauty is indeed the sphere of unfettered contemplation and reflection; beauty conducts us into the world of ideas, without however taking us from the world of sense, as occurs when a truth is perceived and acknowledged. This is the pure product of a process of abstraction from everything material and accidental, a pure object free from every subjective barrier, a pure state of self-activity without any admixture of passive sensations. There is indeed a way back to sensation from the highest abstraction; for thought teaches the inner sensation, and the idea of logical or moral unity passes into a sensation of sensual accord. But if we delight in knowledge we separate very accurately our own conceptions from our sensations; we look upon the latter as something accidental, which might have been omitted without the knowledge being impaired thereby, without truth being less true. It would, however, be a vain attempt to suppress this connection of the faculty of feeling with the idea of beauty, consequently, we shall not succeed in representing to ourselves one as the effect of the other, but we must look upon them both together and reciprocally as cause and effect. In the pleasure which we derive from knowledge we readily distinguish the passage from the active to the passive state, and we clearly perceive that the first ends when the second begins. On the contrary, from the pleasure which we take in beauty, this transition from the active to the passive is not perceivable, and reflection is so intimately blended with feeling that we believe we feel the form immediately. Beauty is then an object to us, it is true, because reflection is the condition of the feeling which we have of it; but it is also a state of our personality (our Ego) because the feeling is the condition of the idea we conceive of it: beauty is therefore doubtless form, because we contemplate it, but it is equally life because we feel it. In a word, it is at once our state and our act. And precisely because it is at the same time both a state and an act, it triumphantly proves to us that the passive does not exclude the active, neither matter nor form, neither the finite nor the infinite; and that consequently the physical dependence to which man is necessarily devoted does not in any way destroy his moral liberty. This is the proof of beauty, and I ought to add that this *alone* can prove it. In fact, as in the possession of truth or of logical unity, feeling is not necessarily one with the thought, but follows it accidentally; it is a fact which only proves that a sensitive nature can succeed a rational nature, and *vice versâ*; not that they co-exist, that they exercise a reciprocal action one over the other; and, lastly, that they ought to be united in an absolute and necessary manner. From this exclusion of feeling as long as there is thought, and of thought so long as there is feeling, we should on the contrary conclude that the two natures are incompatible, so that in order to demonstrate that pure reason is to be realized in humanity, the best proof given by the analysis is that this realization is demanded. But, as in the realization of beauty or of aesthetic unity, there is a real union, mutual substitution of matter and of form, of passive and of active, by this alone is proved the compatibility of the two natures, the possible realization of the infinite in the finite, and consequently also the possibility of the most sublime humanity.

Henceforth we need no longer be embarrassed to find a transition from dependent feeling to moral liberty, because beauty reveals to us the fact that they can perfectly coexist, and that to show himself a spirit, man need not escape from matter. But if on one side he is free, even in his relation with a visible world, as the fact of beauty teaches, and if on the other side freedom is something absolute and supersensuous, as its idea necessarily implies, the question is no longer how man succeeds in raising himself from the finite to the absolute, and opposing himself in his thought and will to sensuality, as this has already been produced in the fact of beauty. In a word, we have no longer to ask how he passes from virtue to truth which is already included in the former, but how he opens a way for himself from vulgar reality to aesthetic reality, and from the ordinary feelings of life to the perception of the beautiful.

Letter XXVI

I have shown in the previous letters that it is only the aesthetic disposition of the soul that gives birth to liberty, it cannot therefore be derived from liberty nor have a moral origin. It must be a gift of nature; the favor of chance alone can break the bonds of the physical state and bring the savage to duty. The germ of the beautiful will find an equal difficulty in developing itself in countries where a severe nature forbids man to enjoy himself, and in those where a prodigal nature dispenses him from all effort; where the blunted senses experience no want, and where violent desire can never be satisfied. The delightful flower of the beautiful will never unfold itself in the case of the Troglodyte hid in his cavern always alone, and never finding humanity outside himself; nor among nomads, who, travelling in great troops, only consist of a multitude, and have no individual humanity. It will only flourish in places where man converses peacefully with himself in his cottage, and with the whole race when he issues from it. In those climates where a limpid ether opens the senses to the lightest impression, whilst a life-giving warmth develops a luxuriant nature, where even in the inanimate creation the sway of inert matter is overthrown, and the victorious form ennobles even the most abject natures; in this joyful state and fortunate zone, where activity alone leads to enjoyment, and enjoyment to activity, from life itself issues a holy harmony, and the laws of order develop life, a different result takes place. When imagination incessantly escapes from reality, and does not abandon the simplicity of nature in its wanderings: then and there only the mind and the senses, the receptive force and the plastic force, are developed in that happy equilibrium which is the soul of the beautiful and the condition of humanity.

What phenomenon accompanies the initiation of the savage into humanity? However far we look back into history the phenomenon is identical among all people who have shaken off the slavery of the animal state: the love of appearance, the inclination for dress and for games.

Extreme stupidity and extreme intelligence have a certain affinity in only seeking the real and being completely insensible to mere appearance. The former is only drawn forth by the immediate presence of an object in the senses, and the second is reduced to a quiescent state only by referring conceptions to the facts of experience. In short, stupidity cannot rise above reality, nor the intelligence descend below truth. Thus, in as far as the want of reality and attachment to the real are only the consequence of a want and a defect, indifference to the real and an interest taken in appearances are a real enlargement of humanity and a decisive step towards culture. In the first place it is the proof of an exterior liberty, for as long as necessity commands and want solicits, the fancy is strictly chained down to the real: it is only when want is satisfied that it develops without hinderance. But it is also the proof of an internal liberty, because it reveals to us a force which, independent of an external substratum, sets itself in motion, and has sufficient energy to remove from itself the solicitations of nature. The reality of things is effected by things, the appearance of things is the work of man, and a soul that takes pleasure in appearance does not take pleasure in what it receives but in what it makes.

It is self-evident that I am speaking of aesthetical evidence different from reality and truth, and not of logical appearance identical with them. Therefore if it is liked it is because it is an appearance, and not because it is held to be something better than it is: the first principle alone is a play, whilst the second is a deception. To give a value to the appearance of the first kind can never injure truth, because it is never to be feared that it will supplant it—the only way in which truth can be injured. To despise this appearance is to despise in general all the fine arts of which it is the essence. Nevertheless, it happens sometimes that the understanding carries its zeal for reality as far as this intolerance, and strikes with a sentence of ostracism all the arts relating to beauty in appearance, because it is only an appearance. However, the intelligence only shows this vigorous spirit when it calls to mind the affinity pointed out further back. I shall find some day the occasion to treat specially of the limits of beauty in its appearance.

It is nature herself which raises man from reality to appearance by endowing him with two senses which only lead him to the knowledge of the real through appearance. In the eye and the ear the organs of the senses are already freed from the persecutions of nature, and the object with which we are immediately in contact through the animal senses is remoter from us. What we see by the eye differs from what we feel; for the understanding to reach objects overleaps the light which separates us from them. In truth, we are passive to an object: in sight and hearing the object is a form we create. While still a savage, man only enjoys through touch merely aided by sight and sound. He either does not rise to perception through sight, or does not rest there. As soon as he begins to enjoy through sight, vision has an independent value, he is aesthetically free, and the instinct of play is developed.

The instinct of play likes appearance, and directly it is awakened it is followed by the formal imitative instinct which treats appearance as an independent thing. Directly man has come to distinguish the appearance from the reality, the form from the body, he can separate, in fact he has already done so. Thus the faculty of the art of imitation is given with the faculty of form in general. The inclination that draws us to it reposes on another tendency I have not to notice here. The exact period when the aesthetic instinct, or that of art, develops, depends entirely on the attraction that mere appearance has for men.

As every real existence proceeds from nature as a foreign power, whilst every appearance comes in the first place from man as a percipient subject, he only uses his absolute sight in separating semblance from essence, and arranging according to subjective law. With an unbridled liberty he can unite what nature has severed, provided he can imagine his union, and he can separate what nature has united, provided this separation can take place in his intelligence. Here nothing can be sacred to him but his own law: the only condition imposed upon him is to respect the border which separates his own sphere from the existence of things or from the realm of nature.

This human right of ruling is exercised by man in the art of appearance; and his success in extending the empire of the beautiful, and guarding the frontiers of truth, will be in proportion with the strictness with which he separates form from substance: for if he frees appearance from reality, he must also do the converse.

But man possesses sovereign power only in the world of appearance, in the unsubstantial realm of imagination, only by abstaining from giving being to appearance in theory, and by giving it being in practice. It follows that the poet transgresses his proper limits when he attributes being to his ideal, and when he gives this ideal aim as a determined existence. For he can only reach this result by exceeding his right as a poet, that of encroaching by the ideal on the field of experience, and by pretending to determine real existence in virtue of a simple possibility, or else he renounces his right as a poet by letting experience encroach on the sphere of the ideal, and by restricting possibility to the conditions of reality.

It is only by being frank or disclaiming all reality, and by being independent or doing without reality, that the appearance is aesthetical. Directly it apes reality or needs reality for effect, it is nothing more than a vile instrument for material ends, and can prove nothing for the freedom of the mind. Moreover, the object in which we find beauty need not be unreal if our judgment disregards this reality; for if it regards this the judgment is no longer aesthetical. A beautiful woman, if living, would no doubt please us as much and rather more than an equally beautiful woman seen in painting; but what makes the former please men is not her being an independent appearance; she no longer pleases the pure aesthetic feeling. In the painting, life must only attract as an appearance, and reality as an idea. But it is certain that to feel in a living object only the pure appearance requires a greatly higher aesthetic culture than to do without life in the appearance.

When the frank and independent appearance is found in man separately, or in a whole people, it may be inferred they have mind, taste, and all prerogatives connected with them. In this case the ideal will be seen to govern real life, honor triumphing over fortune, thought over enjoyment, the dream of immortality over a transitory existence.

In this case public opinion will no longer be feared, and an olive crown will be more valued than a purple mantle. Impotence and perversity alone have recourse to false and paltry semblance, and individuals as well as nations who lend to reality the support of appearance, or to the aesthetic appearance the support of reality, show their moral unworthiness and their aesthetical impotence. Therefore, a short and conclusive answer can be given to this question— how far will appearance be permitted in the moral world? It will run thus in proportion as this appearance will be aesthetical, that is, an appearance that does not try to make up for reality, nor requires to be made up for by it. The aesthetical appearance can never endanger the truth of morals: wherever it seems to do so the appearance is not aesthetical. Only a stranger to the fashionable world can take the polite assurances, which are only a form, for proofs of affection, and say he has been deceived; but only a clumsy fellow in good society calls in the aid of duplicity and flatters to become amiable. The former lacks the pure sense for independent appearance; therefore he can only give a value to appearance by truth. The second lacks reality, and wishes to replace it by appearance. Nothing is more common than to hear depreciators of the times utter these paltry complaints— that all solidity has disappeared from the world, and that essence is neglected for semblance. Though I feel by no means called upon to defend this age against these reproaches, I must say that the wide application of these criticisms shows that they attach blame to the age, not only on the score of the false, but also of the frank appearance. And even the exceptions they admit in favor of the beautiful have for their object less the independent appearance than the needy appearance. Not only do they attack the artificial coloring that hides truth and replaces reality, but also the beneficent appearance that fills a vacuum and clothes poverty; and they even attack the ideal appearance that ennobles a vulgar reality. Their strict sense of truth is rightly offended by the falsity of manners; unfortunately, they class politeness in this category. It displeases them that the noisy and showy so often eclipse true merit, but they are no less shocked that appearance is also demanded from merit, and that a real substance does not dispense with an agreeable form. They regret the cordiality, the energy, and solidity of ancient times; they would restore with them ancient coarseness, heaviness, and the old Gothic profusion. By judgments of this kind they show an esteem for the matter itself unworthy of humanity, which ought only to value the matter inasmuch as it can receive a form and enlarge the empire of ideas. Accordingly, the taste of the age need not much fear these criticisms if it can clear itself before better judges. Our defect is not to grant a value to aesthetic appearance (we do not do this enough): a severe judge of the beautiful might rather reproach us with not having arrived at pure appearance, with not having separated clearly enough existence from the phenomenon, and thus established their limits. We shall deserve this reproach so long as we cannot enjoy the beautiful in living nature without desiring it; as long as we cannot admire the beautiful in the imitative arts without having an end in view; as long as we do not grant to imagination an absolute legislation of its own; and as long as we do not inspire it with care for its dignity by the esteem we testify for its works.

Letter XXVII

D o not fear for reality and truth. Even if the elevated idea of aesthetic appearance become general, it would not become so, as long as man remains so little cultivated as to abuse it; and if it became general, this would result from a culture that would prevent all abuse of it. The pursuit of independent appearance requires more power of abstraction, freedom of heart, and energy of will than man requires to shut himself up in reality; and he must have left the latter behind him if he wishes to attain to aesthetic appearance. Therefore, a man would calculate very badly who took the road of the ideal to save himself that of reality. Thus, reality would not have much to fear from appearance, as we understand it; but, on the other hand, appearance would have more to fear from reality. Chained to matter, man uses appearance for his purposes before he allows it a proper personality in the art of the ideal: to come to that point a complete revolution must take place in his mode of feeling, otherwise, he would not be even on the way to the ideal. Consequently, when we find in man the signs of a pure and disinterested esteem, we can infer that this revolution has taken place in his nature, and that humanity has really begun in him. Signs of this kind are found even in the first and rude attempts that he makes to embellish his existence, even at the risk of making it worse in its material conditions. As soon as he begins to prefer form to substance and to risk reality for appearance (known by him to be such), the barriers of animal life fall, and he finds himself on a track that has no end.

Not satisfied with the needs of nature, he demands the superfluous. First, only the superfluous of matter, to secure his enjoyment beyond the present necessity; but afterward; he wishes a superabundance in matter, an aesthetical supplement to satisfy the impulse for the formal, to extend enjoyment beyond necessity. By piling up provisions simply for a future use, and anticipating their enjoyment in the imagination, he outsteps the limits of the present moment, but not those of time in general. He enjoys more; he does not enjoy differently. But as soon as he makes form enter into his enjoyment, and he keeps in view the forms of the objects which satisfy his desires, he has not only increased his pleasure in extent and intensity, but he has also ennobled it in mode and species.

No doubt nature has given more than is necessary to unreasoning beings; she has caused a gleam of freedom to shine even in the darkness of animal life. When the lion is not tormented by hunger, and when no wild beast challenges him to fight, his unemployed energy creates an object for himself; full of ardor, he fills the re-echoing desert with his terrible roars, and his exuberant force rejoices in itself, showing itself without an object. The insect flits about rejoicing in life in the sunlight, and it is certainly not the cry of want that makes itself heard in the melodious song of the bird; there is undeniably freedom in these movements, though it is not emancipation from want in general, but from a determinate external necessity.

The animal *works*, when a privation is the motor of its activity, and it *plays* when the plenitude of force is this motor, when an exuberant life is excited to action. Even in inanimate nature a luxury of strength and a latitude of determination are shown, which in this material sense might be styled play. The tree produces numberless germs that are abortive without developing, and it sends forth more roots, branches, and leaves, organs of nutrition, than are used for the preservation of the species. Whatever this tree restores to the elements of its exuberant life, without using it or enjoying it, may be expended by life in free and joyful movements. It is thus that nature offers in her material sphere a sort of prelude to the limitless, and that even there she suppresses partially the chains from which she will be completely emancipated in the realm of form. The constraint of superabundance or *physical play* answers as a transition from the constraint of necessity, or of *physical seriousness*, to aesthetical play; and before shaking off, in the supreme freedom of the beautiful, the yoke of any special aim, nature already approaches, at least remotely, this independence, by the *free movement* which is itself its own end and means.

The imagination, like the bodily organs, has in man its free movement and its material play, a play in which, without any reference to form, it simply takes pleasure in its arbitrary power and in the absence of all hinderance. These plays of fancy, inasmuch as form is not mixed up with them, and because a free succession of images makes all their charm, though confined to man, belong exclusively to animal life, and only prove one thing—that he is delivered from all external sensuous constraint without our being entitled to infer that there is in it an independent plastic force.

From this play of *free association* of ideas, which is still quite material in nature and is explained by simple natural laws, the imagination, by making the attempt of creating a free form, passes at length at a jump to the aesthetic play: I say at one leap, for quite a new force enters into action here; for here, for the first time, the legislative mind is mixed with the acts of a blind instinct, subjects the arbitrary march of the imagination to its eternal and immutable unity, causes its independent permanence to enter in that which is transitory, and its infinity in the sensuous. Nevertheless, as long as rude nature, which knows of no other law than running incessantly from change to change, will yet retain too much strength, it will oppose itself by its different caprices to this necessity; by its agitation to this permanence; by its manifold needs to this independence, and by its insatiability to this sublime simplicity. It will be also troublesome to recognize the instinct of play in its first trials, seeing that the sensuous impulsion, with its capricious humor and its violent appetites, constantly crosses. It is on that account that we see the taste, still coarse, seize that which is new and startling, the disordered, the adventurous and the strange, the violent and the savage, and fly from nothing so much as from calm and simplicity. It invents grotesque figures, it likes rapid transitions, luxurious forms, sharply-marked changes, acute tones, a pathetic song. That which man calls beautiful at this time is that which excites him, that which gives him matter; but that which excites him to give his personality to the object, that which gives matter to a *possible plastic operation*, for otherwise it would not be the beautiful for him. A remarkable change has therefore taken place in the form of his judgments; he searches for these objects, not because they affect him, but because they furnish him with the occasion of acting; they please him, not because they answer to a want, but because they satisfy a law which speaks in his breast, although quite low as yet.

Letters on the Aesthetical Education of Man

Soon it will not be sufficient for things to please him; he will wish to please: in the first place, it is true, only by that which belongs to him; afterwards by that which he is. That which he possesses, that which he produces, ought not merely to bear any more the traces of servitude, nor to mark out the end, simply and scrupulously, by the form. Independently of the use to which it is destined, the object ought also to reflect the enlightened intelligence which imagines it, the hand which shaped it with affection, the mind free and serene which chose it and exposed it to view. Now, the ancient German searches for more *magnificent* furs, for more *splendid* antlers of the stag, for more elegant drinking-horns; and the Caledonian chooses the prettiest shells for his festivals. The arms themselves ought to be no longer only objects of terror, but also of pleasure; and the skilfully-worked scabbard will not attract less attention than the homicidal edge of the sword. The instinct of play, not satisfied with bringing into the sphere of the necessary an aesthetic superabundance for the future more free, is at last completely emancipated from the bonds of duty, and the beautiful becomes of itself an object of man's exertions. He adorns himself. The free pleasure comes to take a place among his wants, and the useless soon becomes the best part of his joys. Form, which from the outside gradually approaches him, in his dwelling, his furniture, his clothing, begins at last to take possession of the man himself, to transform him, at first exteriorly, and afterwards in the interior. The disordered leaps of joy become the dance, the formless gesture is changed into an amiable and harmonious pantomime, the confused accents of feeling are developed, and begin to obey measures and adapt themselves to song. When, like the flight of cranes, the Trojan army rushes on to the field of battle with thrilling cries, the Greek army approaches in silence and with a noble and measured step. On the one side we see but the exuberance of a blind force, on the other the triumph of form, and the simple majesty of law.

Now, a nobler necessity binds the two sexes mutually, and the interests of the heart contribute in rendering durable an alliance which was at first capricious and changing like the desire that knits it. Delivered from the heavy fetters of desire, the eye, now calmer, attends to the form, the soul contemplates the soul, and the interested exchange of pleasure becomes a generous exchange of mutual inclination. Desire enlarges and rises to love, in proportion as it sees humanity dawn in its object; and, despising the vile triumphs gained by the senses, man tries to win a nobler victory over the will. The necessity of pleasing subjects the powerful nature to the gentle laws of taste; pleasure may be stolen, but love must be a gift. To obtain this higher recompense, it is only through the form and not through matter that it can carry on the contest. It must cease to act on feeling as a force, to appear in the intelligence as a simple phenomenon; it must respect liberty, as it is liberty it wishes to please. The beautiful reconciles the contrast of different natures in its simplest and purest expression. It also reconciles the eternal contrast of the two sexes in the whole complex framework of society, or at all events it seeks to do so; and, taking as its model the free alliance it has knit between manly strength and womanly gentleness, it strives to place in harmony, in the moral world, all the elements of gentleness and of violence. Now, at length, weakness becomes sacred, and an unbridled strength disgraces; the injustice of nature is corrected by the generosity of chivalrous manners. The being whom no power can make tremble, is disarmed by the amiable blush of modesty, and tears extinguish a vengeance that blood could not have quenched. Hatred itself hears the delicate voice of honor, the conqueror's sword spares the disarmed enemy, and a hospitable hearth smokes for the stranger on the dreaded hillside where murder alone awaited him before.

In the midst of the formidable realm of forces, and of the sacred empire of laws, the aesthetic impulse of form creates by degrees a third and a joyous realm, that of play and of the appearance, where she emancipates man from fetters, in all his relations, and from all that is named constraint, whether physical or moral.

If in the dynamic state of rights men mutually move and come into collision as forces, in the moral (ethical) state of duties, man opposes to man the majesty of the laws, and chains down his will. In this realm of the beautiful or the aesthetic state, man ought to appear to man only as a form, and an object of free play. To give freedom through freedom is the fundamental law of this realm.

The dynamic state can only make society simple possibly by subduing nature through nature; the moral (ethical) state can only make it morally necessary by submitting the will of the individual to the general will.

The aesthetic state alone can make it real, because it carries out the will of all through the nature of the individual. If necessity alone forces man to enter into society, and if his reason engraves on his soul social principles, it is beauty only that can give him a social *character*; taste alone brings harmony into society, because it creates harmony in the individual. All other forms of perception divide the man, because they are based exclusively either in the sensuous or in the spiritual part of his being. It is only the perception of beauty that makes of him an entirety, because it demands the co-operation of his two natures. All other forms of communication divide society, because they apply exclusively either to the receptivity or to the private activity of its members, and therefore to what distinguishes men one from the other. The aesthetic communication alone unites society because it applies to what is common to all its members. We only enjoy the pleasures of sense as individuals, without the nature of the race in us sharing in it; accordingly, we cannot generalize our individual pleasures, because we cannot generalize our individuality. We enjoy the pleasures of knowledge as a race, dropping the individual in our judgment; but we cannot generalize the pleasures of the understanding, because we cannot eliminate individuality from the judgments of others as we do from our own. Beauty alone can we enjoy both as individuals and as a race, that is, as representing a race. Good appertaining to sense can only make one person happy, because it is founded on inclination, which is always exclusive; and it can only make a man partially happy, because his real personality does not share in it. Absolute good can only render a man happy conditionally, for truth is only the reward of abnegation, and a pure heart alone has faith in a pure will. Beauty alone confers happiness on all, and under its influence every being forgets that he is limited.

Taste does not suffer any superior or absolute authority, and the sway of beauty is extended over appearance. It extends up to the seat of reason's supremacy, suppressing all that is material. It extends down to where sensuous impulse rules with blind compulsion, and form is undeveloped. Taste ever maintains its power on these remote borders, where legislation is taken from it. Particular desires must renounce their egotism, and the agreeable, otherwise tempting the senses, must in matters of taste adorn the mind with the attractions of grace.

Duty and stern necessity must change their forbidding tone, only excused by resistance, and do homage to nature by

Letters on the Aesthetical Education of Man

a nobler trust in her. Taste leads our knowledge from the mysteries of science into the open expanse of common sense, and changes a narrow scholasticism into the common property of the human race. Here the highest genius must leave its particular elevation, and make itself familiar to the comprehension even of a child. Strength must let the Graces bind it, and the arbitrary lion must yield to the reins of love. For this purpose taste throws a veil over physical necessity, offending a free mind by its coarse nudity, and dissimulating our degrading parentage with matter by a delightful illusion of freedom. Mercenary art itself rises from the dust; and the bondage of the bodily, at its magic touch, falls off from the inanimate and animate. In the aesthetic state the most slavish tool is a free citizen, having the same rights as the noblest; and the intellect which shapes the mass to its intent must consult it concerning its destination. Consequently, in the realm of aesthetic appearance, the idea of equality is realized, which the political zealot would gladly see carried out socially. It has often been said that perfect politeness is only found near a throne. If thus restricted in the material, man has, as elsewhere appears, to find compensation in the ideal world.

Does such a state of beauty in appearance exist, and where? It must be in every finely-harmonized soul; but as a fact, only in select circles, like the pure ideal of the church and state — in circles where manners are not formed by the empty imitations of the foreign, but by the very beauty of nature; where man passes through all sorts of complications in all simplicity and innocence, neither forced to trench on another's freedom to preserve his own, nor to show grace at the cost of dignity.

Made in the USA
Monee, IL
08 February 2023

27308232R10075